Lawyer-Proof Your Life

A Do-It-Yourself Guide to Saving Time, Saving Money, and Avoiding Lawsuits

Robert E. Bauman JD

BANYAN HILL

Banyan Hill Publishing
P.O. Box 8378
Delray Beach, FL 33482
Tel.: 866-584-4096
Email: http://banyanhill.com/contact-us
Web: http://banyanhill.com

ISBN: 978-0-692-46551-6

Lawyer-Proof Your Life

*A Do-It-Yourself Guide to Saving Time,
Saving Money, and Avoiding Lawsuits*

Robert E. Bauman JD

About the Author

Robert E. Bauman JD

Bob Bauman, legal counsel to Banyan Hill (previously The Sovereign Society), served as a member of the U.S. House of Representatives from 1973 to 1981 representing the First District of Maryland. He is an author and lecturer on many aspects of wealth protection, offshore residence and second citizenship.

A member of the District of Columbia Bar, he received his juris doctor degree from the Law Center of Georgetown University in 1964. He has a B.S. degree in International Relations from the Georgetown University School of Foreign Service (1959) and was honored with GU's Distinguished Alumni Award.

He is the author of *The Gentleman from Maryland* (Hearst Book Publishing, NY); and the following books, all published by Banyan Hill Publishing: *The Passport Book: The Complete Guide to Offshore Residency, Dual Citizenship and Second Passports*; *Where to Stash Your Cash Legally: Offshore Financial Centers of the World*, *The Offshore Money Manual*; editor of *Forbidden Knowledge*; *Swiss Money Secrets*; and *Panama Money Secrets*. His writings have appeared in *The Wall Street Journal*, *The New York Times*, *National Review*, and other publications.

TABLE OF CONTENTS

INTRODUCTION

In America, we have one of the best legal systems in the world. Yet, if you're like most people, you're overwhelmed and intimidated by that system. You may have been indoctrinated to believe that there's no way you can deal with the complexities of this system by yourself, so you don't even try.

You feel helpless — and you resent the "fact" that you have to hire a high-priced lawyer every time you need to sign a simple piece of paper. Well, I'm here to prove to you that's not the case.

You don't have to have a law degree to handle most legal procedures. In fact, most of the legal minutia filling countless computer files in any lawyer's office reflects work done and decisions made not by a lawyer, but by the lawyer's secretary, an office paralegal or even a bright young student intern.

The vast majority of an attorney's law practice consists of routine paperwork that any reasonably bright person can master in a short time. Computers loaded with specialized legal software programs now spit out hundreds of standard forms of wills, contracts and premarital agreements, for example — into which the variables of each client's name and relevant facts are inserted at appropriate places by a clerk. You can do the same thing for yourself with a few inexpensive forms you can download from the Internet or buy at your neighborhood office supply store — and with the help of *Lawyer-Proof Your Life*.

Granted, you may run into some complicated legal situations that will require the expertise of a professional. But even then, this book will help by giving you the information you need to realistically assess your own position, and to understand the recommendations and actions of your attorney.

Here's just a small sampling of what you'll learn:

- Your rights and legal obligations concerning marriage, divorce, alimony, and child support;
- How to secure your assets by incorporating your business or forming a partnership;

- How to control distribution of your property after death and to protect your loved ones with different types of wills, trusts, and guardianships;

- What to do if you're involved in a civil lawsuit — whether you're the injured party or the one being sued;

- What to do if you're arrested or charged with a crime;

- How to protect yourself if you're buying, selling, renting, or renting out property;

- What to do if you're in an auto or other accident;

- How to handle driving violations and problems with automobile insurance;

- Everything you need to know before drawing up or signing a contract of any kind;

- Your rights as a consumer;

- How to deal with the government in disputes over Social Security, disability payments, or workman's compensation;

- And much, much more!

My goal here is to help keep you in control of your own life, and your own business and financial dealings. Just think of this book as the legal equivalent of a first-aid manual. You've learned how to self-medicate your sore throat and bandage minor scrapes and burns without first graduating from medical school. Now I'm going to teach you how to bind up your own legal wounds and ... lawyer-proof your life.

Bob Bauman

Robert E. Bauman JD
Washington, D.C. Bar #966838
U.S. House of Representatives, 1973-1981
Maryland State Senate, 1971-1973

CHAPTER 1:
THE TROUBLE WITH LAWYERS

According to the American Bar Association, in 2014 there were 1,281,432 lawyers in the United States, a number that represents over 70% of all the lawyers in the world. This represents an increase of over 100% from the 1980 total of 574,810, and an incredible 150% increase from the 1970 total of 326,842.

Where do all these attorneys in the United States find work?

The *Lawyer Statistical Report* of the American Bar Foundation provides some answers.

Three-fourths (75%) of America's lawyers are in private practice, some in small, one-person offices and some in much larger law firms. About 8% of the legal profession works for government agencies, another 8% work for private industries and associations as lawyers or managers, about 1% work for legal aid associations or as public defenders, representing those who cannot afford to pay a lawyer, and 1% are in legal education. Approximately 5% of the nation's lawyers are retired or inactive.

Not surprisingly, the single greatest glut within this nationwide lawyer explosion is located in the nation's capital — the Washington, D.C. area, which is the site of the greatest concentration of lawyers working in any single city. Across the Potomac River in Arlington County, Virginia, nearly 6,000 lawyers make their homes. That equals about 30 lawyers for every 1,000 citizens — the nation's highest per capita ratio. New York City comes in second in total number of attorneys with nearly 50,000 and Los Angeles County has the most located in any single county — about 40,000.

Miraculously, 348 mainly rural American counties in states like Nevada, Utah and Nebraska manage to get by without having a single lawyer in their midst. America has 361 lawyers for every 100,000 people, compared to Britain with 94 per 100,000, 33 per 100,000 in France and a mere seven per 100,000 in Japan.

All these lawyers have been very busy.

According to the National Conference of State Courts, more than 16.6 million civil cases entered the state court system in 2005, the most recent year for which numbers are available. This was by no means a record and represented nearly 500,000 fewer incoming cases than in 2003 and the second consecutive year of decline. Adjusting for population growth, the resulting aggregate rate of just over 5,500 cases for every 100,000 residents of the United States is nearly identical to the rate in 1996.

Only two states, Maryland and Virginia, as well as the District of Columbia reported rates above 10,000 per 100,000 residents. Maryland's rate was by far the highest at over 17,000 incoming civil cases per 100,000 state residents.

These dramatic numbers clearly demonstrate how Americans have been led to believe that a lawyer's assistance to be essential when faced with a legal problem of almost any kind. After all, what does the average person know about the mysteries of the law? That's why attorneys are required to go to law school, isn't it — so they can master the intricacies of such a vast, complex field of knowledge?

A common misconception is that all legal matters are "serious" by their very nature. Thus, the conventional wisdom when a legal problem arises, is "Don't try to do it yourself — get an attorney." This theme has been repeated so often (usually by lawyers), it has been reduced to a modern adage: "The person who acts as his or her own attorney has a fool for a client."

All this "get-a-lawyer" propaganda is the product of a tacit conspiracy — a quietly organized facade constructed to fool the gullible and impress the uninformed. Lawyers themselves are responsible for this conspiracy. Collectively they have long hidden behind a legal magic curtain, protecting their interests by making "The Law" seem mysterious and beyond the comprehension of mere non-attorney mortals.

American lawyers perpetuate their monopoly by weighing down documents and pleadings with Latin phrases that many don't fully understand. Some case pleadings and court practices are based on procedures that hardly have been altered since King John was forced to sign the Magna Carta in 1215. Under this English and American common law pleading system, technicalities ruled the day. If a lawyer used one wrong phrase, his entire case would be lost, regardless of the merits. Only lawyers who knew the magic formulas could navigate successfully in such a closed system.

To their credit, progressive lawyers joined in reforming this antiquated system over the years. Today, basic points of the law are far less mysterious for anyone with a reasonably capable intellect and a little persistence.

And yet the myth continues — that "laymen cannot understand basic concepts of our legal system without the help of an attorney."

The Paralegal Battle

Lawyers have employed trained paralegals in their offices for many years, depending on them for much of the research, case management and the boring but essential paperwork no attorney enjoys doing.

Several years ago, paralegals sought to establish their own independent offices providing legal forms and advice about where to find answers to legal questions without consulting an attorney. Lawyers and their bar associations launched a fierce attack on the paralegal movement, claiming the paralegals were practicing law without a license.

An early and classic example of the organized bar's attack was a lawsuit filed by the Florida Bar Association against Rosemary Furman, a north Florida paralegal who opened a do-it-yourself legal business in the 1980s. Ms. Furman sold legal forms for wills, name changes and uncontested divorces, servicing mainly poor and illiterate people who could never have afforded to hire an attorney.

In 1984, the Florida Supreme Court put Ms. Furman out of business for "practicing law without a license." Only by the governor's grant of clemency did Ms. Furman avoid her 30-day jail term for contempt of court imposed after she disobeyed an order to stop her paralegal work.

While the Florida lawyers won this battle, they lost the public relations war. CBS television's *"60 Minutes"* featured Ms. Furman, and she became a national martyr of sorts. As one attorney put it, "The Furman case opened the legal profession to further scorn and distrust."

In 1987, the U.S. Supreme Court ruled that secretarial services could answer basic questions about legal forms, as long as only court-approved forms were used. At that time, there were few such forms, but most state courts have now approved forms for divorces, child support, name changes and other simple legal procedures. Non-lawyers can legally advise you on which forms are appropriate for your situation.

The High Cost of Lawyers

The Furman case highlighted another aspect of the lawyer problem — the prohibitive cost of hiring one. Even before O.J. Simpson's highly publicized 1995 murder trial or the unprecedented 1999 establishment of a sexual harassment legal defense fund for then-president of the United States, Bill Clinton, many Americans were well aware that only the rich could afford attorneys — especially at a rate of $500 to $1000 an hour.

Today, far too many lawyers view their clients primarily as a source of revenue, rather than as individuals to whom they owe a sworn duty of scrupulous service. "Billable hours" too often replaces the concept of personal trust and non-conflicting devotion to the client.

Laurence Tribe, noted Harvard University law professor and frequent television "legal expert," billed a client $625 for a one-sentence letter actually written by one of his law students. "It was a very long sentence," Professor Tribe explained shamelessly.

The overbilling trend has gotten worse in recent years. Several prominent attorneys have been charged with cheating clients by overbilling. Maureen Fairchild, a former partner in the leading Chicago law firm of Chapman & Cutler, was accused by attorney discipline authorities of overbilling clients more than $1.3 million by inflating time sheets for herself and lawyers she supervised. Her husband, Gary Fairchild, was dismissed as managing partner of Winston & Strawn in Chicago after that firm accused him of padding his expense account by more than $500,000. And Harvey Meyerson, a once-prominent Wall Street lawyer, was sentenced to 70 months in prison after being found guilty of overbilling clients by more than $2 million.

It is impossible to calculate exactly how widespread this sort of dishonesty and criminal conduct is among lawyers. If you believe that you may be the victim of overbilling, confront your attorney with your suspicions. If you don't get satisfaction, contact your state's bar association.

A Legal Monopoly

Lawyers have a unique monopoly few other professions enjoy. Think about the process: lawyers make the laws (in the U.S. Congress and most state legislatures, the largest single occupational group is lawyers); lawyers, as judges, interpret and apply the laws; and only attorneys are allowed to represent people who find themselves entangled with the same law, (although you can choose to represent yourself). And when it comes to policing the ethical conduct of lawyers, mostly lawyers administer codes of conduct they write themselves, through bar associations and grievance committees they control, usually meeting in secret. Most of these committees have a dismal record of disciplining fellow attorneys.

It's not surprising that this inbred legal system, supposedly designed to "help" and "protect" the people, often winds up hurting them instead. Most of us are familiar with legal horror stories involving people we know — ugly divorce cases, contested wills, bungled medical malpractice and auto accident lawsuits — which not only failed to resolve disputes, but instead resulted in even more personal hardship.

One of the major causes of public distrust of the legal profession is the bar's continued unwillingness to expose attorneys' abuses and the reluctance of judges to disbar, suspend or even publicly reprimand unethical lawyers. One study discovered that 90% of complaints filed by clients against lawyers are never even investigated and much less result in any disciplinary action. Of those client complaints of lawyer misconduct which do prompt official action, fewer than 10% result in an attorney's disbarment and, even then, this mild penalty is usually imposed only for a temporary period of a few months.

Yet clients' complaints grow in number each year, passing 100,000 annually. According to American Bar Association (ABA) statistics, of those clients who sue their former attorneys for legal malpractice, only 37% receive some compensation — usually less than $1,000 — and then only as a result of settling out of court. Of those ex-clients who go to trial, fewer than 2% win in court.

The ABA itself has maintained a "National Lawyer Regulatory Data Bank," which contains the current names, addresses, aliases (yes, aliases!), and violations of about 25,000 lawyers who have run afoul of the law. The ABA has placed its bad lawyer data bank online, at https://www.americanbar.org/groups/professional_responsibility/services/databank.html

Since attorneys are licensed by the 50 states and the District of Columbia, you should also check the Directory of Lawyer Disciplinary Agencies at https://www.americanbar.org/content/dam/aba/administrative/professional_responsibility/2014_directory_disciplinary_agencies_online_092014.authcheckdam.pdf

But is anyone surprised the ABA is restricting availability of the data to state and local lawyer disciplinary authorities? The online information isn't available to the general public — the group containing potential clients most likely in need of information about a lawyer's honesty and integrity. You can, however, still call or write the ABA in Chicago, and they might tell you if your attorney is on the "bad guys" list.

The great majority of lawyers refuse to represent people in cases alleging legal malpractice — not only for fear of being shunned by their fellow attorneys, but because these situations are extremely difficult to prove in court. To win a legal malpractice suit, an ex-client must show that the lawyer was negligent and that the original case would have been won on its merits had the lawyer done his or her job properly. That's a nearly impossible double burden of proof.

Despite lawyers' unwillingness, the number of court decisions reported on such cases is growing each year. And every now and then, justice does triumph. A Houston, Texas, jury awarded $21.7 million in actual and punitive damages for legal malpractice against one of the nation's largest (500+ lawyers)

Chapter 1

and best-connected law firms, Vinson and Elkins. The jury found the firm guilty of running up millions of dollars in unnecessary legal fees while handling the $80 million estate of a deceased Texas oil man, W.T. Moran. The firm also lost millions improperly investing estate assets and delaying settlement of the estate. Furthermore, the firm was found guilty of violating state deceptive advertising laws. Naturally, all those lawyers at Vinson and Elkins have appealed the verdict.

Money Talks

Virtually every attempt to reform the current civil suit system is met with staunch and determined organized resistance by trial lawyers, who contribute massive amounts of political campaign funds to legislators who have the power to enact the needed reform laws. The American Association for Justice (formerly the Association of Trial Lawyers of America [ATLA]) that boasts 56,000 members has given $11,759,320 to 622 political candidates and committees over the last 16 years, 95% to Democrats, since that political party opposes tort law reform and restrictions on unreasonable lawsuits. In the 2014 U.S. federal elections, the trial lawyers donated more than $7 million to various candidates.

Realize there is a lot at stake here: The legal system for redressing civil wrongs (tort suits) cost a whopping $264.6 billion in 2010, which translates to $857 per U.S. person, a 5.1% over 2009. Much of that increase was attributable to the April 2010 Deepwater Horizon drilling rig explosion and resulting oil spill in the Gulf of Mexico. However, that 2010 total was a five-fold increase since 1930. This figure includes judgments, legal fees, court costs, etc. During the 60-year span from 1951 to 2010, the average annual increase in tort cost was 8.7%.

According to an annual study by Tillnghast and Towares Perrin — an international consulting firm — the U.S. suffers the highest tort costs among 12 industrialized western nations, coming in at roughly 2% of the entire gross national product. Consumers then pay for these tort litigation costs through higher product prices and insurance rates.

Choosing a Lawyer

The process of finding a good lawyer is difficult. The best are always busy — and usually very high-priced. Unless you know and trust the advice of someone who has personally been served by a particular attorney and is satisfied enough to make a recommendation, you take your chances when you hire an attorney.

An initial consultation with an attorney may cost relatively little. After that first meeting, however, most attorneys require that their clients pay them a "retainer fee," an up-front payment which can be a considerable amount (possibly $5,000 or more), depending on the legal work proposed. Usually, charges are assessed against the retainer fee at an hourly rate. When the retainer is used up, the client is billed for additional time.

After the initial encounter, too many lawyers follow an unspoken policy of avoiding personal contact with their clients unless absolutely necessary. You may get to know your lawyer's secretary or receptionist far better than you will ever know your lawyer, who seems always to be "in conference" or "in court" or "with a client" — which may be true, or it may mean he or she is on the golf course.

Then there is the problem — seldom discussed openly in legal circles — of the actual competency of those who are already admitted to practice law.

"What?" you say, "Aren't lawyers licensed by the state?" Don't they have to pass a bar examination and be qualified?"

The lawyer-like answer to these questions is, "Yes, and no."

The truth is that most of the 203 ABA-accredited law schools in the United States tend to teach: 1) case law, which is a method devised at Harvard in 1870 for reviewing past court decisions on any given topic, and; 2) abstract legal theory.

Practical legal knowledge, such as counseling clients, dealing with court personnel, research and advocacy skills and developing good legal judgment, is learned almost exclusively on the job. And you may be the one who unknowingly provides the opportunity for an attorney to acquire that needed experience.

Even in established law firms, it is common for a client to meet initially with a well-known senior partner, thus giving the impression that this experienced professional will be doing the work. Instead, a junior attorney new to the firm may, in fact, be responsible for most of the grunt work of your case.

Your success will depend on the junior attorney's abilities, not those of the senior partner you thought you were hiring as your personal advocate. Yes, the senior's signature will be on the papers, but the content will most likely be the product of the junior associate.

That's not the worst possibility, however. A license to practice law allows any attorney to take any case. You can never be sure that the specialized category of law into which your problem fits is one with which your lawyer has experience.

Remember — not all lawyers know about all legal problems and there is no requirement that they be so widely qualified. Nor do all states have "continuing legal education (CLE)" requirements, which are periodic refresher courses designed to keep lawyers up-to-date on the latest developments. Some states have adopted rules allowing lawyers to publicly identify themselves as "specialists," provided they have attended a certain number of classes dealing with that area of the law.

The late Warren Burger, former Chief Justice of the United States Supreme Court, wryly observed, "If law school graduates, like cars, could be recalled for failure to meet commercial standards, the recall rate would be very high…" One of the few attorneys who does specialize in legal malpractice cases, Edward Freidberg of Sacramento, California, is not quite so diplomatic, "I would say that one in four trial lawyers is incompetent or routinely negligent."

To borrow one of those old Latin legal phrases, "*Caveat emptor*" — "Let the buyer beware."

Back Scratching

Most lawyers limit their practice to a defined geographic area within which they constantly work and deal with the same judges, lawyers and officials day after day, year after year. You may be privileged to be Lawyer Smith's client at the moment, but Lawyer Jones, who represents the rotten guy you are suing, has known Lawyer Smith since law school. They go to the same bar meetings, belong to the same clubs and may even socialize on a regular basis. So, long after you and your opponent are no longer fighting in court, these two lawyers will remain friends. The Code of Professional Responsibility governing all lawyers clearly requires each one, as counselor and advocate, to give paramount consideration to his or her client's best interests at all times. And most do. But can all lawyers be depended on to do that? Most opposing lawyers want to maximize cooperation with each other in order to fight another day — long after your case is settled.

If this back-scratching fact of legal life makes you uncomfortable as a potential client of Lawyer Smith or Lawyer Jones, it should. This intramural professional coziness is a point of which you should not only be aware, but one you should carefully check as it applies to your situation.

When You Need a Lawyer

I must admit, as an attorney myself, I have been rather tough on my colleagues with these remarks. My criticisms certainly do not apply to all lawyers.

There are many situations which can have serious legal ramifications on your life — so serious that the best course of action is to obtain the professional guidance of a qualified attorney. If you think you need a lawyer, get referrals from trusted acquaintances, check the Internet under "Lawyer Referral Services," or contact the office of your state or local bar association, which also can be found online.

CHAPTER 2:
SOURCES, COURTS AND LEGAL RESEARCH

A**ll citizens of the United States and all foreign nationals within U.S. borders are governed by two different and distinct bodies of law: federal laws enacted by the U.S. Congress in Washington, D.C., and state laws adopted by legislatures in the 50 state capitals. Federal laws generally have nationwide authority, but the power and efficacy of state laws end at each state's borders.

A Dual System of Laws

Some areas of the law are governed almost exclusively by federal law. These include interstate commercial regulation, foreign policy, international trade and dealing with illegal immigration, regardless of the impact such matters may have on individual states.

Almost all criminal acts are strictly matters of state jurisdiction, except when the crimes are committed in federally controlled areas, such as within the U.S. National Parks system or on a U.S. military base. Other legal issues, such as the allowable weight, height, width and length of commercial trucks traveling on state roads, are also covered primarily by state law.

Areas of the law that are governed by both federal and state law fall under concurrent jurisdiction. For example, when a crime is committed by an active duty armed services member on a military base, the military court has jurisdiction. But if a service member commits a crime away from a military base, a state court has jurisdiction.

Most jurisdictional conflicts are resolved by the courts themselves based on the doctrine of comity, meaning that as a matter of courtesy and goodwill, but not as a matter of right, one court will voluntarily defer to the jurisdiction of another court. For instance, in cases involving the sale or possession of illegal drugs by active military personnel, many state courts defer to military courts on the grounds that the illegal use of drugs is of vital concern to the military branch of government, outweighing the need of a state to enforce its criminal law.

What this short course in the duality of our legal systems requires of you, as the potential researcher of legal issues, is constant awareness of which system governs the field of law in which your research should be conducted.

Always ask yourself first, "Is my problem a matter of federal or state law, or both?" The answer to that question will determine exactly where you should start your research.

Constitutions, Statutes and Codes

Most people are aware of the United States Constitution, the basic charter creating our system of government and guaranteeing our individual rights. Adopted in 1789, it has been amended 27 times — most recently in 1992.

And there is an interesting story about the 27th Amendment.

The 27th Amendment to the U.S. Constitution reads:

No law, varying the compensation for the services of Senators and Representatives, shall take effect, until an election of Representatives shall have intervened.

The long history of the 27th Amendment is curious and unprecedented. The amendment was first drafted by James Madison in 1789 and proposed by the 1st Congress in 1789 as part of the original Bill of Rights.

This proposed amendment was left in limbo when only six states ratified it during the period in which the first ten amendments, the Bill of Rights, were ratified by the requisite three-fourths of the states. The amendment was largely neglected for the next two centuries; Ohio was the only state to approve the amendment in that period, ratifying it in 1873.

In 1982, while doing research for a paper in a government class that he was taking at the University of Texas at Austin, Gregory Watson discovered this unratified constitutional amendment that had been pending ratification by the states since the 1st Congress in 1789.

Watson set out to secure the amendment's incorporation into the Constitution. In 1982 he began a letter-writing campaign to strategically targeted state legislatures and officials. Initial reaction was swift. Over the next ten years, the legislatures of more states ratified Madison's original proposal. On May 19, 1992, the Archivist of the United States certified that the amendment's ratification was completed, with the legislatures of more than 38 states ratifying it.

Watson was called "the stepfather of the 27th Amendment" and is the subject of a chapter in the book, *Citizen Democracy: Political Activists in a Cynical Age* (1999).

The Bill of Rights

The first 10 amendments adopted in 1791 comprise what is known as the Bill of Rights, guaranteeing, among other things, freedom of religion, the right to bear arms, protection against illegal search and seizure, the right to a speedy trial and a trial by jury, and the prohibition of cruel and unusual punishment. (For more on this topic see Chapter 12.)

The Constitution outlines the three branches of government. Article I creates the U.S. Congress, the legislative branch; Article II, the president and the executive branch; Article III, creates the Supreme Court and the judicial branch.

Each state also has its own constitution, which cannot conflict with the U.S. Constitution, but sometimes is more liberal or different in scope, such as in the area of equal rights for women and men.

Both the federal and state governments annually publish their own separate series of law books containing the official statement of the laws governing that state. These official versions are called statutes or codes — the words are synonymous. When the published books also include court cases explaining the meaning of the various sections of the law, they are called annotated statutes or annotated codes.

On the federal level, statutory law can be found in the official *"U.S. Statutes at Large,"* which are rarely used for research, and the frequently used *United States Code* (U.S.C.), published by West Publishing Company (now a part of Thomson Reuters) with official cooperation and approval. The U.S.C. contains more than 100 volumes, each of which is divided into sections. The codes are grouped under various topics, such as "Transportation" or "Veterans," and each topic often requires several volumes.

Each part of the code is identified by a specific citation. For example, the citation "18 U.S.C. sec. 1963 (1993)" refers to the "Racketeering and Corrupt Organizations Act (RICO)." "18" represents the U.S.C. volume number, "1963" designates the section, and "(1993)" indicates the publication year of either the volume or, in this case because of the date, the pocket part in the back of that volume. (Each U.S.C. volume has a supplementary pocket part in its back which is changed each year to update any changes in the law and add new cases.) All federal court cases which have interpreted that section of the U.S.C. will be listed directly following the exact language of the law in force at the time of the printing.

The *United States Code Annotated*® (USCA) contains all the laws in the USC, (Titles 1-50 and the Constitution), plus judicial cases. It mirrors the official text of the USC published by the Office of the Law Revision Counsel of the House of Representatives. Because it is available by subscription in a constantly updated form on the Internet, it is used most often by attorneys. It can be downloaded in pdf form for a price from publishers Thomson Reuters at: http://legalsolutions.thomson-reuters.com/law-products/Court-Rules/United-States-Code-Annotated-USCA/p/100028559

State statutory laws can be found in similar sets of annotated codes that are published by each state, also arranging the topics into volumes and sections that include interpretive state court case decisions. State codes are often published under such titles as *West's Annotated Florida Code* or *Vernon's Annotated Statutes*.

A typical example of a state code citation is "Mo. Ann. Stat. sec. 513.623 (Vernon 1997)." This citation refers to a Missouri law governing the forfeiture to the state of property used in criminal activities. There is no volume number in this example because specific sections of many state codes, although printed in many volumes, are identified by consecutive numbers under topic headings ("Health," "Banking," or "Highways," for example), with the first three or four numbers (here "513") designating the law topic, and the numbers after the decimal point (here "623") indicating the section.

Federal and state codes have indexes (the last few volumes of the set) in which you can locate the section number references by searching under the subject that interests you. Keep in mind that code and statute indexes are notorious for grouping topics under headings a lay person would not ordinarily think appropriate, but lawyers apparently would. Thus, if you want to know about the crime of "trespass," you may have to look under the general heading of crimes. The point is, don't give up.

There are federal and state laws, but don't forget that local laws or municipal ordinances may be imposed by county and city governments. These laws usually govern limited regional topics, such as zoning, public works, street paving, sewer and water use, area real estate restrictions, and building code requirements. The content of local laws may be most important to understanding your legal problem, so don't overlook them when doing research, if you think they may apply.

The Common Law

There is another very important body of law to which judges often look for guidance — the common law. This body of judge-made law originated in 12th Century England, when judges in the relatively new Royal Courts were constantly faced with novel questions for which they had no precedents (prior similar cases) to guide them. With no precedents or statutory law, the judges applied the principles of established social customs, common sense and their own native wisdom to decide cases. One by one, these case decisions, often written down and reported to other courts, became precedents themselves, guiding later justices faced with similar issues.

This tradition of later courts following prior decisions is known as the doctrine of *stare decisis*, Latin for "follow decisions." It means that once a certain issue of law has been decided, especially by a higher court of appeal or the highest court in a judicial system, all other courts are obliged to decide future cases involving the same issue the same way. This provides stability and continuity of the law and it is supposed to prevent judges from changing the interpretation of the law with every case.

This does not mean that judges are blind to changes in society and must repeatedly adopt outdated ideas. It does mean that once the United States Supreme Court has ruled on a matter, all other courts must follow that precedent. But even the Supreme Court can change with the times.

For example, in 1897 the Supreme Court ruled in *Plessy* v. *Ferguson* that it was constitutional for whites and blacks to have segregated public facilities and services, if they were "separate but equal" — which they rarely were. In 1954, in *Brown* v. *Board of Education*, the Supreme Court reversed itself, holding educational segregation to be unconstitutional since racially segregated school systems were inherently unequal.

Even though legislated statutory law often changes the common law, courts continue to look to common law precedents to define the application of law to modern conduct. Thus, common law remains an important source of law in America.

The Federal Court System

Article III of the U.S. Constitution created the U.S. Supreme Court as the highest federal court — the final arbiter of the meaning of our Constitution and laws. All other federal and state courts must follow the Supreme Court, unless Congress and the states adopt an amendment to the Constitution overruling the Court — which has been done, but rarely.

Article III also gave Congress the power to create "inferior courts." These include the U.S. Circuit Courts of Appeal, just below the Supreme Court level, divided into nine "circuits" of several states each. There is also a U.S. Circuit Court for the District of Columbia, hearing cases from the capital city, and a "Federal Circuit Court of Appeals" (also located in Washington, D.C.), with special limited jurisdiction to hear direct appeals of federal administrative and other agencies decisions. These appeals courts consider important questions of federal and constitutional law appealed from lower federal and state courts, acting as a screen before cases are accepted for decision by the Supreme Court.

Below the U.S. Circuit Courts of Appeal are U.S. District Courts, which are the primary federal trial courts. There is at least one in each state, and when there is more than one district Court in a state, each is subdivided into geographic areas designated as "northern district" or "middle district" or "eastern district," as appropriate. As part of the U.S. District Court system special U.S. Bankruptcy Courts handle all bankruptcy cases in the nation.

There are also federal courts with specialized jurisdictions, including the Tax Court, the Customs Court, the Court of Customs and Patent Appeals, the Court of Claims, the Court of Veterans Appeals and the Court of Military Appeals.

State Courts

Totally apart from the federal court system, each of the 50 states has a state high court, often known as the State Supreme Court or the State Court of Appeals. Each state also has a series of circuit appeals courts based on geographic regions, and below them, local trial courts, usually limited in jurisdiction to one county or a major city.

Most states and some counties and cities also have specialized courts with limited powers over certain areas of the law, such as minor crimes, small claims, traffic violations and landlord-tenant disputes. Cities and towns usually have municipal court systems, which handle only local matters.

How to Find the Law

In the more than two centuries of their existence, the federal and state courts have already answered hundreds of thousands, if not millions, of questions concerning the law. The first step in research is to find out whether the questions in your case have been answered before.

You must find a case or cases that match your situation exactly, or nearly so, to find out what the law says about your problem. Maybe your case is so unique that no such prior case has been decided in your state — but perhaps it has in another state. That case will give you an idea of how it might go in your state court.

As stated previously, once a court decides a legal issue, the case usually (but not always) sets a precedent for future similar cases. This doctrine requires courts to follow previous judicial decisions once made, unless the ordinary principles of justice require otherwise, or unless the legislature has changed the law since the prior case was decided.

With so many courts handing down so many decisions, and with laws changing all the time, how do you find that one certain case or group of cases bearing on your legal problem?

First, in the United States Code (U.S.C.) or in a state annotated code, find the exact section of federal or state law that applies to your problem. Remember there may be several applicable sections.

Just as there are published federal and state statutes or codes which give the statutory law, there are several published federal and state "reporter series," which report court decisions interpreting the law. There are reporter series containing U.S. Supreme Court decisions, as well as multi-state regional reporters which contain decisions of courts in your state's region.

Printed under each section of the U.S.C. and of each state annotated code will be multiple citations giving the case names (and reference numbers used in the reporter series) interpreting the meaning of that section. Each "cite," as it is called, contains a brief summary paragraph of the case, and a reference to exactly where in the federal or state reporter series the case can be found. If the case summary sounds like it may have an important impact on your legal problem, you should find it and read it. A case citation looks like this:

Miller v. *United States*, 78 U.S. 268 (1871)

The underlined names are the parties to the suit. In the above citation, a man named "Miller" sued the United States government, contesting as unconstitutional a law passed by Congress allowing federal confiscation of the property of Confederate soldiers and sympathizers during the Civil War, which the Court upheld as a proper exercise of the federal government's war powers.

The letters "U.S." indicate the reporter series name for U.S. Supreme Court case decisions, "78" the volume number and "268" the page number on which the case begins. The year the case was decided is shown by "(1871)." All reporter series follow this formula — first volume number, then reporter series name, then page number and date.

Similar reporter series exist for U.S. Circuit Courts, called the "*Federal Reporter Series.*" Example:

United States v. *Statewide Auto Parts, Inc.*,
971 F.2d 896 (2d Cir. 1992)

In this case, "971" is the volume number in the second ("F.2d") series of "*Federal Reporter*" volumes, "896" the first case page, and the information in parentheses indicates that the

Second Circuit Court of Appeals (comprised of New York, Vermont, and Connecticut) decided the case in 1992. Often you will see the first page number followed by another page number, as in "971 F.2d 896, 902." The second page number is the exact page at which the quotation to which the citation refers appears in the decision. This is a uniform rule in all citations, so if you want to go right to the page with the interesting quote, turn to the second page number.

Reports of cases in U.S. District Courts are reported in the "*Federal Supplement*" reporter series. A typical citation reads as follows:

> *United States* v. *Reckemeyer,*
> 628 F.Supp. 616 (E.D. Va. 1986)

Here again, "628" is the volume of the "*Federal Supplement*" reporter series, "616" the initial page number, and in parentheses we see that the case was decided by the district court in the Eastern District of Virginia in 1986. The fact that "F.Supp." is not followed by a "2d" means it is the first series.

Generally, case decisions of State Supreme Courts (and some state lower courts) are reported in several regional series of state reporters also published by West Publishing Co., with titles such as "*Atlantic*" (A.2d), '*Northeastern*" (N.E.2d), "*Pacific*" (p.2d) — each reporter series covering the courts in the various states in those geographic regions. Placement of volume, page, and date cites are the same as in the federal reporter series.

Many of more recent cases are available by subscription online from Thomson Reuters publishers.

Here is an example of a case citation to be found in the "*Southern Reporter*" second series, decided by the Florida Supreme Court in 1985:

> *Johnson* v. *Davis,*
> 480 So.2d 625 (Fla. 1985)

Codes of Regulations

Federal and state codes of regulations are rules written by government bureaucrats under broad rule-making authority granted to them by the legislators. Although these rules are not actual laws passed by Congress or a state legislature, they do have the force of law. In effect, Congress or a state legislature says to executive branch officials, "This issue is too complex for us to write a complete law covering every possibility. You work out the details and issue implementing regulations to do what we generally want done."

Much of the current federal and state control over individual citizens comes in the form of these "regulations" and concern matters such as the environment, occupational safety, or education and health — to name just a few.

When a new or revised regulation is proposed by the federal government, it is first published in the Federal Register (FR) for public review and comment. When the rule becomes final and attains the force of law, it appears in the multivolume Code of Federal Regulations (CFR).

Each state has a similar set of official rules and regulations as well. Most annotated codes or statutes have section footnotes cross-referencing applicable sections of the CFR or state regulations, but these are rarely complete. Always check the indexes of the CFR or your state code of regulations under the topical headings of interest to you.

Law Encyclopedias

Although they are not official publications, each state usually has an established publication series, which is an encyclopedia of the state law. The series name varies from state to state, and many are published by West Publishing Company or other legal publishers. They have titles such as *Florida Jurisprudence* (Fla. Jur.) or the *Maryland Law Encyclopedia* (MLE).

The encyclopedias come in many volumes, sometimes in second series. Legal topics are listed alphabetically and the index tells you the volume location of your particular topic.

Under each topic heading, you will find extensive annotated essays concerning all aspects of the law on that one subject, giving citations to all the federal and state court cases and statutes relevant to the topic. These encyclopedias are a good starting point for researching matters governed mostly by state law because they give the reader a comprehensive and detailed overview of the subject. They also report federal laws and cases which have an impact on state law.

There are several comparable law encyclopedia series covering federal law and federal case decisions. The best known is probably *Corpus Juris Secundum* (C.J.S.), an ancient series which includes annually updated state law summaries and case references. CJS is written by and for lawyers, and its language is not always easy to comprehend, even for lawyers.

Chapter 2

Friendly Libraries

You can bet these statutes, codes, case reporter series, codes of regulations and law encyclopedias rarely appear on bestseller lists. You won't even find these books in your local public library, unless that library is one of the few — usually located in the largest cities — designated by federal law as a repository for federal documents. And then that library may offer only the federal volumes, not the state.

One place you will find these books is your county or city court house library. Your local public library staff can tell you where the public law library is located — it's not always in the court house — and other information about its use. You may want to be prepared to make copies of any information you want to keep as none of these libraries lend books.

Law school libraries also contain all the federal and state reference books discussed here. Such libraries generally are not open to the public, but a polite request at the front desk will usually gain admittance. You may even ask questions to a certain degree.

Students in law school usually have unlimited use of West Publishing Company's national legal computer system known as "*Westlaw*." As a promotional gimmick, West gives law students unlimited access during the course of their law studies, undoubtedly achieving their goal of hooking them for life on the comprehensive "Westlaw" reporting system.

No wonder. "Westlaw," through the use of a personal computer and modem, offers immediate Internet access to every page of every series of books mentioned in this chapter and hundreds of thousands of additional publications. Just type the command "FIND" followed by a case name or citation and, within seconds, it's on your screen. Or just type a word or phrase ("breach of promise," for example), and "Westlaw" will deliver every case on that topic within a selected database.

Another Internet source of information for the public and for legal professionals is FindLaw, a free resource that includes online case law, free state codes, free federal codes, free legal forms and articles. See http://www.findlaw.com/

What to Look For

A proper study and assessment of the facts of your case may immediately indicate your chance of prevailing or it may show a need for further investigation before a reliable opinion can be formulated. Whenever you have a legal matter you want to resolve (with or without the assistance of a lawyer), first write down the five "w's" of the case — the who, what, where, when, and why.

Next, decide what the major issues are and between which parties they exist. Then turn to the topic chapter in this book that best suits your legal situation. I have made it fairly simple to find the correlation between the facts of a potential case and the applicable law by grouping common legal topics under everyday headings — such as "Transportation Law," "Family Law," "Civil Rights," etc.

Although there are times when the assistance of a lawyer may be necessary, there are many more times when such help is not needed. Now that you know how to do your own legal research, you should be able to make that decision intelligently. At the very least, your research will give you a better understanding of the problem before you approach an attorney — a definite advantage when entering a law office for the first time.

About Legal Forms

Throughout this book we provide samples of commonly used legal forms that should give you a good idea of the necessary elements. These forms, however, are generic in nature and may or may not fit the facts and applicable law of your particular situation. If you have any doubts, check with the clerk of the court in which your document is to be filed or contact a lawyer.

If you need additional forms, *West's Pleading and Practice Forms* is a well-respected multi-volume series of thousands of forms used in daily legal practice and in pleadings in state and federal courts. The series can be found at any law library and has a good topical index and is kept up-to-date with a cumulative annual pocket parts in the back of each volume.

There are many Internet companies that sell downloadable legal forms for prices some consider to be far too high. Rather than buying these forms, go to www.google.com and search for free forms.

CHAPTER 3:
FAMILY LAW

Family law covers a multitude of topics centering on the basic unit of society — the family. Among others, these topics include marriage, separation, divorce, alimony and child support, adoption, name changes, proof of paternity and the rights of unmarried persons living together.

At the outset, understand that domestic relations (especially those involving family disputes) are perhaps the most contentious and unpleasant situations with which the law must deal. Because of emotional and personal factors, this is one legal area in which the dispassionate and objective assistance of a trained family lawyer is almost always essential.

This is especially so because most domestic quarrels also involve property rights and settlements. State laws governing domestic matters are complicated, and the parties to the dispute (especially in a divorce) are usually angry, confused and incapable of thinking clearly. The two people headed for a separation or divorce often make irrational decisions based on momentary emotional responses of guilt or revenge — and they soon live to regret their actions.

That's why both parties in a domestic dispute should be represented by good lawyers who are able to offer objective advice and reasonable counsel. In many states, it is unlawful for the same lawyer to represent both parties in matters such as separation, divorce or premarital agreements. Whether per mitted or not, it is never a good idea because of the conflict of interest it causes.

Premarital Agreements

A premarital agreement is a contract entered into by a couple prior to their marriage, setting forth exactly how their property will be divided if the marriage ends either by divorce or death. Years ago, many courts would not honor such agreements if made contingent on divorce, because public policy viewed the contract as promoting marriage discord and divorce. Today, state courts take differing stands on interpreting the details of such agreements, but most find them to be mutually binding when freely entered into after full disclosure by both parties of their assets, both current and potential.

If you or your proposed spouse (or both) have a large amount of property and wealth (or may later acquire it), it is wise to work out a premarital agreement, with each of you represented by separate lawyers — regardless of how rosy your present relationship may be. The contract should be written in simple language, so that both of you can easily understand what you are signing. (See a sample on the next page.)

Marriage

Reduced to its bare legal meaning, marriage is a binding, enforceable contract between two parties, encouraged by society and officially approved and regulated by the state.

In order to have a valid marriage, both parties must be mentally capable of fully understanding what they are doing and of giving their informed consent. They must also be physically capable of fulfilling the procreative purposes of marriage. A marriage may be voided later if, at the time of the ceremony, either party was intoxicated or otherwise mentally impaired or under duress, or if either party is sterile, impotent or pregnant, and that fact was unknown to the other party.

Each state's requirements differ, but most specify a minimum age (usually 18, but in some cases 16) for both the husband and wife, although marriage below the minimum age is usually allowed with parental or court consent.

There are classes of people who, for the most part, are by law not allowed to marry: a parent and child; a great grandparent or grandparent and great grandchild or grandchild; a brother and sister (including a half-brother and half-sister); an uncle and niece; and an aunt and nephew. Many states forbid marriage between first cousins, and some between a stepparent and stepchild, and between a father-in-law and daughter-in-law and a mother-in-law and son-in-law.

Premarital Agreement

THIS AGREEMENT is entered into this [date day of month], 20__ , between [name of first party] and [name of second party].

WHEREAS, the parties contemplate legal marriage under the laws of the State of [state name where the marriage will take place]; and whereas it is their mutual desire to enter into this agreement so that each party will continue to own and exercise control over his/her own property; and whereas neither party desires that their present separate financial interests be changed by their marriage;

NOW, THEREFORE, THE PARTIES AGREE AS FOLLOWS:

All property which belongs to each of the above parties shall remain, now and forever, their personal and separate property, including all interest, rents, and profits that may accrue from said property, and said property shall remain forever free of claim by the other.

Both parties shall continue to have the full right and authority, in all respects the same as each would have if not married, to use, enjoy, sell, manage, lease, give, and convey all property as may presently belong to him or her.

In the event of a separation or divorce, the parties shall have no right against each other by way of claims for spousal support, alimony, maintenance, compensation, or division of any separately owned property existing as of [this date].

In the event of separation or divorce, marital property acquired after marriage shall nevertheless remain subject to division, either by agreement or judicial determination.

In the event of the death of either party, the surviving party agrees that the distribution of the deceased's property shall be governed solely by the Last Will and Testament of the deceased party.

This agreement shall be binding upon and inure to be beneficial to both parties, their heirs, successors, assigns, and personal representatives.

Both parties acknowledge that they have entered into this agreement after full disclosure of all property owned by each of them.

This agreement shall be enforced in accordance with the laws of the State of [state where couple will reside].

Signed this *date* day of *month*, *year*.

Witness' signature _____	*First party's signature* _____
Witness	First Party
Witness' signature _____	*Second party's signature* _____
Witness	Second Party

Most state courts find premarital agreements to be mutually binding when freely entered into after full disclosure by both parties of their assets.

Chapter 3

Same Sex Marriage

"Same-sex marriage" obviously is a marriage between two persons of the same sex. The issue is a divisive political issue in the United States and became prominent in U.S. politics in the 1990s and continues to this day.

In June 2015, the high court ruled, 5-4, in *Obergefell* v. *Hodges*, an opinion authored by Justice Anthony Kennedy, that: "The right to marry is a fundamental right inherent in the liberty of the person. Under the Due Process and Equal Protection Clauses of the Fourteenth Amendment couples of the same sex may not be deprived of that right and that liberty."

Obergefell v. *Hodges* combined four challenges to state same-sex marriage bans, from Kentucky, Tennessee, Ohio and Michigan. Framed in broad terms the case addressed the question of whether the federal constitution required all states to license same-sex marriages and to recognize those marriages if they were performed elsewhere.

The legal issues surrounding same-sex marriage in the United States are complicated by the nation's federal system of government I described earlier in Chapter One.

Traditionally, the federal government did not attempt to establish its own definition of marriage. Any marriage recognized by a state was recognized by the federal government, even if that marriage was not recognized by one or more other states. This was the case with state anti-miscegenation laws that prohibited interracial marriage before they were ruled unconstitutional by the U.S. Supreme Court in *Loving* v. *Virginia*, 1967.

In 1996, the U.S. Congress by large margins in both houses, adopted, and President Bill Clinton, signed the Defense of Marriage Act (DOMA). This Act explicitly defined "marriage" as a union of one man and one woman for the purposes of federal law. (See 1 USC § 7) Sec. 3 of the Act directed that no action or agency of the U.S. federal government could recognize same-sex marriage as legal and it also allowed states to refuse to recognize same-sex marriages granted under the laws of other states.

In 2011, although President Obama had endorsed DOMA as a candidate, his attorney general, Eric Holder, took the unusual step of announcing that he had concluded the Act was unconstitutional, that although the administration would continue to enforce the law while it existed, it would no longer defend the law in court. In *United States* v. *Windsor* (2013), the U.S. Supreme Court declared DOMA unconstitutional under the Due Process Clause of the Fifth Amendment.

As of 2015, in the United States same sex marriages were legal in Alaska, Arizona, California, Colorado, Connecticut, Delaware, Florida, Hawaii, Idaho, Illinois, Indiana, Iowa, Kansas, Maine, Maryland, Massachusetts, Minnesota, Montana, Nevada, New Hampshire, New Jersey, New Mexico, New York, North Carolina, Oklahoma, Oregon, Pennsylvania, Rhode Island, South Carolina, Utah, Vermont, Virginia, Washington, West Virginia, Wisconsin, and Wyoming.

In is worth noting that in 2010, 40 states had constitutional amendments or laws explicitly barring the recognition of same-sex marriage, confining civil marriage to a legal union between a man and a woman. Forty-three states had statutes restricting marriage to two persons of the opposite sex, including some of those that had created legal recognition for same-sex unions under a name other than "marriage." A small number of states banned any legal recognition of same-sex unions that would be equivalent to civil marriage.

Many of these laws had been adopted in state-wide referenda. In every state where the issue was put before the voters, gay marriage was rejected. In 2008, California passed its ban, known as Proposition 8, and voters in Maine overturned a state law allowing same-sex marriages in 2009. By May 2012, voters in 30 states had approved such amendments.

In spite of these expressions of the popular will of voters, as of June 2015, only 13 state bans remained in effect with five others in court. In every case federal and states courts had overruled same sex marriage bans; none had been repealed by legislatures.

Although the Supreme Court decision in *Obergefell* v. *Hodges* decided the issue nationally as a matter of law, it did not end the controversy. Complicated issues will need to considered in what may be a host of lawsuits, determining what First Amendment religious rights opponents of same sex marriage have in refusing to cooperate with the ruling.

State Law Governs

The general rule is that each state must recognize as valid a marriage legally contracted in another state, but some do not if the sole reason for the out of state marriage was to get around a state law; making such marriages illegal.

Before a couple can marry, most states require them to apply for a marriage license, usually at the county court house. A license must be used within a defined time period (30 to 90 days on average) or it expires. Many states also require a premarital blood test for certain sexually transmitted diseases (STDs) and for rubella in females. Some states have a two-to seven-day waiting period between license application and issuance, while others (Nevada) have no waiting period.

The wedding ceremony must be performed by a person legally authorized to do so — a minister, priest, rabbi, judge, or justice of the peace — who officially reports the marriage to the state. One or two witnesses are required. Contrary to the popular belief fostered by old Hollywood movies, ship captains do not generally have the power to perform marriages.

Sixteen states, Alabama, Colorado, Georgia, Idaho, Iowa, Kansas, Montana, New Hampshire, New Mexico, Ohio, Oklahoma, Pennsylvania, Rhode Island, South Carolina, Texas, Utah and the District of Columbia permit and recognize common law marriages, but with varying definitions and restrictions. Such a marriage results when the parties, although not formally wed, demonstrably intend to marry, treat each other and present themselves to the public as though married, live together for a minimum period of time and share each other's property and earnings.

Such marriages are recognized in other states if they occur in the jurisdictions named above. Obviously, it is far better to formalize such relationships, thus guarding the legal rights of both parties as well as the rights of any children born of the union. This is especially so to protect pension or Social Security survivors benefits, life insurance proceeds or other inheritances.

The law permits only one legal spouse at a time. Anyone who marries without first obtaining a legal divorce from the first spouse is guilty of bigamy, a crime in most states and possibly an actionable civil suit for the persons wronged by the bigamist partner.

There was a time earlier in this century when the law considered a husband and wife, once married, to be one person for many legal purposes — they could not sue each other — property belonged to the party who provided the funds for it (usually the working husband), and each spouse had a right to the services of the other. Spouses could not testify against each other in court.

Today, every jurisdiction recognizes, where appropriate, the independence of each marriage partner and the individual property rights of each and many states now allow one spouse to testify in all judicial proceedings involving the other.

Annulment

An annulment is a declaration by a court that a marriage was invalid "from the beginning" (*ab initio* in Latin) because of some impediment or problem.

Many factors can support an annulment, among them fraud or deceit that wrongfully induced one party to enter into the marriage, such as concealing a prior marriage, impotency or sterility, or failing to honor a commitment to convert to the other spouse's religion. Lack of mental capacity and duress are also possible grounds for annulment. A person who marries under the legal age can personally assert that fact as grounds for an annulment and so can the minor's parents.

Courts will not usually grant an annulment unless it is sought within a reasonably short period of time after the marriage date, any lengthy time lapse being viewed as acquiescence of the complaining partner.

Separation

To the casual observer, a separation, either voluntary or involuntary, occurs when a married couple no longer lives together, often as a prelude to a divorce. This may be because one spouse deserts the other, or because the couple desires a trial period apart to decide if divorce is advisable for them.

Although they are not free to marry again, there is a major change in their legal relationship. To protect both parties, that change should be formalized, usually in a jointly negotiated separation agreement. This document governs the obligations and rights of each party, such as temporary alimony (spousal support), child support, custody and visitation rights, and economic and other living arrangements. A court can formalize such an agreement by its order, usually as part of an involuntary separation, but most such documents are by contract between the parties, negotiated between the attorneys for each.

Depending on the degree of personal acrimony between the spouses, this can be a tricky and painful event, especially if children are involved. This is an instance where a detached and experienced lawyer for each party can be especially helpful — both exploring any possibility of reconciliation, and also assuring neither spouse is taken advantage of by the other.

Divorce   Because marriage is a social institution with origins in formal religion and protected by the laws of the state, it was for many years very difficult to obtain a legal end to its existence. At one time, "until death do us part" was more than just ritual language in the marriage ceremony.

A divorce is a legal declaration by a court that a valid marriage is officially terminated in the eyes of the state. Except for the obligations the court orders as part of the divorce decree, child support or alimony being most common, each party's obligations to the other end, and they are both free to marry again.

When divorce laws originally were adopted, they emphasized fault as the only basis for dissolving a marriage, such as adultery, physical or mental cruelty, desertion or abandonment, nonsupport or gross neglect, alcoholism or other drug addiction, impotence, insanity or conviction of a felony with a prison sentence of more than a year. In all such cases, the innocent spouse was the only one who could initiate the divorce. About one-third of the states still require a showing of some sort of fault in order to obtain a divorce.

A dozen or so states have abolished the fault concept. No-fault divorces commonly use phrases such as "irreconcilable differences" or "irretrievable breakdown" as grounds for the termination of the marriage. Usually, the parties separate and live apart for some period of time, and the court will grant the divorce based on this mutually agreed upon separation.

In the majority of states, both fault and no-fault grounds support a divorce request. Even though the no-fault concept has gained wide acceptance, the misconduct of one or the other spouse still may have a major influence on how a court will decide other issues, such as child custody and support, alimony, and property settlements.

The majority of divorces granted today are uncontested divorces, with the parties settling their property and child custody differences even before the divorce complaint is filed.

Divorce is governed by state law and, in the great majority of states, a party to a divorce action must be a resident of the state for a minimum period of time, ranging from six months to two years. Only in a few states (such as Nevada) are "quickie" divorces allowed, but running off to one of these states or "south of the border" in Mexico may not guarantee the validity of your divorce — especially when your irate spouse brings your so-called "decree" before a court in your home state.

The U.S. Supreme Court ruled in 1951 that each state must recognize a valid divorce granted by another state. But they also held in 1957 that in order to dispose of both spouses' property rights, each spouse must be resident within the court's jurisdiction. This means that the validity of a divorce decree and property settlements granted in one state can be contested by a party in another state on grounds the decree was invalid under the granting state's law, or that one party was not properly within the court's jurisdiction.

THE CASE OF THE THRIVING THOROUGHBRED

Mary and John have decided to end their marriage of six years. Mary, whose hobby has been raising thoroughbred horses, contends that her star yearling, Native Territory, does not qualify as community property. She insists that she bought the racehorse with income from a trust fund set up by her parents. However, her soon-to-be ex-husband, John, claims the couple's joint personal and investment income enabled Mary to purchase the horse. With race winnings in the bank and the Triple Crown approaching, deciding who owns the horse means big money, even if split 50/50. A judge will demand clear proof from reliable financial records showing the exact origin of Native Territory's purchase money, and, thus, the thoroughbred's rightful owner shall be determined.

In Arizona, California, Idaho, Louisiana, New Mexico, Nevada, Texas, Washington, and Wisconsin, state law imposes the concept of community property, meaning that any property (including income) acquired by either spouse during marriage becomes joint property of both. In these states, the community property figures largely in any divorce property settlement.

Alimony

Spousal support paid to one spouse by the other before or after the divorce becomes final is called alimony. The concept grew out of the common law theory that a husband has a continuing duty to support his wife. Today, although it is still a rare case, a wife may be ordered by a court to pay alimony to her husband, depending on their relative economic and other circumstances. The U.S. Supreme Court has ruled that alimony laws must apply equally to both husbands and wives, in order to be constitutional.

In awarding alimony, a court looks at the relative financial condition of each party, his and her age and station in life, earning capacities, and work abilities — both present and future. Aside from an award of alimony, the court may also divide existing property (such as autos, antiques, personal property), giving one spouse the marital home, the other the vacation retreat — or even ordering the sale of real estate with the proceeds to be split.

Child Support & Custody

Far too often, blindly embittered parties to a pending divorce use minor children as legal pawns to satisfy their own spousal hatreds. Child custody is the one aspect of divorce that usually engenders the greatest heat and the most problems – many lawyers find this difficult to handle because of the personal acrimony and heartbreak involved.

Although in former times the mother was usually favored, today the standard test for deciding child custody is what constitutes the best interests of the child. The factors a court considers include the age and sex of the child; the wishes he or she expresses (especially by an older child); the interaction of the child with the parent or siblings; conditions of the home, school, and community, as well as the mental and physical health of all concerned parties.

In the best situation, parents decide upon a monthly amount of child support to be paid, usually by the husband to the wife, for each minor child. This figure is then incorporated into the court's divorce decree, thus giving it the force of law. Failure to pay may subject the parent to contempt of court, jail time and attachment of any assets, such as bank accounts and property.

If there is disagreement over the amount of support, the court looks to the parent's ability to pay and the child's needs including food, shelter, clothing, and other necessities. Often, courts also impose support obligations for educational, medical and other special expenses for each child.

Unlike alimony, which may continue for any period of time the court orders, child support usually ends when the child reaches 18 years of age. In a few states, 19 is the cut-off age, or when the child becomes self-supporting or marries.

A divorce decree also includes terms governing a parent's child visitation rights, the rights of grandparents and methods by which the terms of the decree can be modified in the future, if need be.

Enforcement of Court Decrees

It does little good for a court to issue decrees if they cannot be enforced — especially when the welfare of impoverished women and children are involved. Yet the problem of "deadbeat dads" has become a national scandal, with some runaway fathers constantly moving across state lines in order to avoid obligations following a divorce. Every time the ex-husband moves to a new state, the ex-wife has to start all over again seeking payment through that state's court system.

In response to estimates of billions of dollars in unpaid child support decrees, both state and federal laws have been toughened to make collection easier. Many states have begun to jail parents who fail to pay after due notice, and some revoke the parent's professional, motor vehicle driver's, or other state issued licenses. If a parent owes more than $2,500 in court-ordered back child support, that parent's U.S. passport is automatically revoked and will not be reinstated until proof of payment shows in state records.

On the federal level, Congress authorized the U.S. Internal Revenue Service and other federal agencies to withhold income tax refunds or benefits (such as veteran's pensions) from parents who are delinquent in their court-ordered child support payments, directing the money to the ex-spouse or child instead. Federal government employees, who were previously exempt from attachment, can now have up to 60% percent of their salaries garnished for child support payments in arrears.

Tracking Down a "Deadbeat Dad"

State laws differ in how they treat situations involving "deadbeat dads" who fail to make court-ordered alimony or child support payments. The act of nonpayment violates a court decree, and, in some states, creates a continuing lien on the delinquent parent's paycheck, bank accounts, and real property. Usually, the state's attorney or the social services department is charged with collecting back payments. Courts routinely order employers to deduct a portion of a deadbeat parent's paycheck and turn it over to the local welfare or social services office, which, in turn, pays the custodial parent. Courts can also issue a "show cause order" against the non-payer and, after a hearing, hold him in contempt of court and jail him until compliance.

Filing bankruptcy does not discharge obligations of alimony or child support; nor does fleeing the state. Since many deadbeat parents attempt to escape their responsibility by crossing state lines, all states now have adopted a version of the "Uniform Reciprocal Enforcement of Support Act (URESA)." This law allows court orders for child support and alimony in one state to be quickly enforced in the courts of other states. If you are owed back payments of alimony or child support, first contact the attorney who handled your divorce. He or she will file a formal complaint in the court that originally issued the decree. The state's attorney or the social services department will pursue the delinquent parent as allowed by law. Private attorneys may also be commissioned by the court to pursue non-payers. It's always wise to personally follow-up with the state agency or court-appointed official that's handling your case.

Unmarried Households

In 2006, a survey reported that for the first time traditional marriage had ceased to be the preferred living arrangement in the majority of U.S. households. The shift, reported by the U.S. Census Bureau in its 2005 American Community Survey, indicated that marriage did not figure in nearly 55.8 million American family households, or 50.2%.

More than 14 million of these households were headed by single women, another five million by single men, while 36.7 million belonged to a category described as "nonfamily households," a term that experts said referred primarily to gay or heterosexual couples cohabiting out of formal wedlock. In addition, there were more than 30 million unmarried men and women living alone, who are not categorized as families, the Census Bureau reported. By comparison, the number of traditional households with married couples at their core stood at slightly more than 55.2 million, or 49.8% of the total.

Unmarried Partners

In 1976, a California court held in the "palimony" case of *Marvin* v. *Marvin*, 18 Cal. 3d 660, that actor Lee Marvin had entered into a contract with his girlfriend, singer Michelle Triola, who gave up her professional career to live with Marvin. They never married, but when they broke up seven years later, she sued claiming he had promised financial support and sharing of both their earnings and property — in return for which she had given up her promising professional career, the proverbial "best years of her life."

The court said any time a party to such an arrangement can satisfactorily prove such a contract was entered into, and what the intended terms were, then it would be enforceable if breached, like any contract. Many other "Marvin" cases have since been heard, some successfully, some not. But it puts a premium on the advice, *"Always get it in writing."* To help you get it in writing, we have included a basic Cohabitation Agreement, a contract that can be revised to meet your situation.

A written cohabitation agreement is a reliable way to protect yourself from the uncertainties of living together and sharing expenses without being married.

In most cases, unmarried couples must depend on contracts between themselves, including mutual durable powers of attorney or mutual powers of attorney for health care — documents that provide for future circumstances in a formal way. Title to real estate and personal property, including bank accounts, can be acquired as joint tenants with the right of survivorship.

This means that in the event of death, the surviving partner automatically becomes the owner of the entire interest, without any need for the property to go through probate proceedings, although estate taxes may be due. Of course, mutual wills are also effective, though they require probate, and an unmarried

A written cohabitation agreement is a reliable way to protect yourself from the uncertainties of living together and sharing expenses without being married.

Cohabitation Agreement

THIS AGREEMENT is entered into this *date* day of *month*, *year*, between *name of first party* and *name of second party* who presently reside in the County of *name of county*, in the State of *name a of state*.

WHEREAS, the parties wish to live together in a relationship similar to matrimony, but do not wish to be bound by the statutory or common-law provisions relating to marriage, it is hereby agreed that the parties to this agreement shall live together for an indefinite period of time subject to the following terms and conditions:

1. Property: Any real or personal property acquired by either party during the relationship shall be considered to be each party's separate property. All property listed on the attached pages is made a part of this agreement by reference. The property now and hereinafter belongs to the party under whose name it is listed prior to the making of this agreement. All listed property is and shall continue to be the separate property of the person who now owns it. All property received by either party by gift or inheritance during the relationship shall be the separate property of the party who receives it.

2. Income: All income earned or accumulated during the relationship shall be maintained in one fund out of which all debts and expenses arising during the existence of this union shall be paid.

3. Termination: The relationship may be terminated at the sole will and decision of either party, expressed by a written notice given to the other party.

4. Modification: This agreement may be modified by an agreement in writing signed by both parties, with the exception that no modifications may decrease the obligations that may be imposed regarding any children born of this union.

5. Application of Law: The validity of this agreement shall be determined solely under the laws of the State of *name of state where parties reside*.

6. Claims Waived: Neither party shall maintain any action or claim against the other party for support, alimony, compensation, or for rights to any property existing prior to this date, or acquired on or subsequent to the date of termination.

7. Free Act of Parties: The parties enter into this agreement of their own will and accord without reliance on any other inducement or promise,

8. Signed this *date* day of *month*, 20*year*.

Witness signature _____   *First party's signature* _____
Witness   First Party

Witness sign _____   *Second party's Signature* _____
Witness   Second Party

partner may be named as the beneficiary of the other partner's life insurance policy. In most major cities, there are now domestic relations attorneys specializing in joint legal arrangements governing the rights of unmarried couples.

Legally establishing the paternity of a child allows a mother to bring further legal action requiring the father to pay child support. Decades ago, the most notorious paternity lawsuits involved public figures or movie stars, such as Charlie Chaplin or Errol Flynn. Hollywood types presumably could be made to pay dearly for their indiscretions.

Paternity & Legitimacy

Today, both state and federal governments have a hand in making a father pay support for an illegitimate child. Under the "Aid for Dependent Children Act (AFDC)," Congress gave each state federal funding to support poor children, but the state must also seek out and force the true fathers to pay back the money government advances for their children. Even though the AFDC program is administered by welfare agencies noted for their bureaucracy, millions of dollars are collected annually from fathers, and part of the collection process now includes proof of paternity.

The easiest method of proof of paternity is to get the man to admit in writing his fathering of the child. But if it becomes an issue in court, with modern scientific methods, including blood type matching, human leukocyte antigen (HLA) and deoxyribonucleic acid (DNA) tests, experts can prove a child's paternity with 99.9% accuracy. It is hardly like the "old days" when a jury was forced to consider circumstantial evidence of "who slept with whom when" from eyewitnesses to supposedly clandestine events.

The illegitimacy of a child born "out of wedlock" was at one time not only treated as a social stigma, but it created legal impediments to inheritance and other family rights of that child.

Today, most states recognize rights of an illegitimate child as equal to those of a legitimate child, including support from the father, inheritance from his estate, ability to sue for his wrongful death and to share in death benefits like workmen's compensation and Social Security.

Adoption

Adoption completely severs the legal relationship created at birth between a child and his or her biological parents. By court decree, it is replaced by the same relationship between the child and persons who are not the natural parents. The adoptive parents assume all rights and duties the natural parents had, and the child assumes the legal position of a blood descendant.

In America, adoption is controlled by the laws of each state, which tend to be similar. Prospective parents file a petition with the appropriate court seeking approval to adopt a named child, setting forth their qualifications and ability to act as parents. A hearing is held to determine the adoption, at which time the court wants to know if the natural parents have consented to the petition and, if not, if they have been given official notice of the hearing and its purpose. (A natural parent can lose his or her right to a child by abandonment or by voluntary relinquishment.)

To complete the adoption, the child's birth certificate is reissued in the new name and all record of the natural parents or the adoption are permanently sealed. Only in the most extraordinary circumstances will a court overturn an adoption once completed.

The Adoption Process

Finding an eligible child is the first, and often most difficult, step of the adoption process. Since every state requires adoption agencies to be licensed, the best place to start is with your local social services department, who can refer you to qualified adoption agencies in your area. Pro-life organizations are also a good source of leads on adoptive children.

In recent years, adoption agencies have begun specializing in children from China, Russia, Eastern European nations, and South America. These are often legitimate operations, but the international aspect can make adoption more costly and more complicated legally.

Most adoptions involve an adult married couple and an infant or young child. Here's how the process usually works: 1) Prospective parents (or their attorney) file a petition with the appropriate state court, requesting permission to adopt a named child and setting forth their parental qualifications; 2) A hearing is held on the petition to determine the child's situation and the approval of the natural parents; and 3) The court issues an adoption decree, changing the child's name and ordering a new birth certificate. Usually, all files regarding the adoption are sealed.

State laws are strict in forbidding the opening of sealed adoption records. There may be criminal penalties for violating such adoption secrecy laws. If you desire information regarding an adoption, first consult an attorney or one of the organizations that promotes such information seeking.

Whether or not a parent can be held liable for personal injuries or property damage caused by his or her minor child depends on state law. Usually a parent is not liable for a child's negligence or simple carelessness. But if injury or damage results from a child's willful misconduct, the parent may well be liable.

Parental Responsibility

Even in such cases, most states limit liability to a relatively small amount — $1,000 to $5,000. In states with what is known as a permissive use statute, parents are liable for any injury caused by a teenager using the family automobile. In other states, they are liable only if the child was using the car for a purpose directed by the parent (such as a trip to the grocery store).

There are times when a parent can be held liable for failure to supervise a child who, as a result, causes harm — for example, if a mother fails to discipline a five-year-old who has been swinging a stick at other kids in the park for 15 minutes before using it to destroy the sight in another child's eye.

In most states, a minor child can sue a parent for any intentional wrong committed to him or her, including unreasonable punishment amounting to child abuse. As a general rule, a child cannot sue a parent for failure to supervise or adequately protect the child from himself. In two recent Florida court decisions, the judge allowed a minor child to sue his or her parents for what amounted to "divorce," granting custody to adult couples the child designated as better suited to care for him or her.

Most states hold a spouse liable for debts incurred by the other spouse if the items purchased are classed as necessities of life (meaning food, housing, clothing, utilities, medical treatment, and children's education). As long as there is no separation or divorce, this spousal obligation continues. Some states view a spouse as an agent of the other spouse when making purchases of this nature. Similarly, parents can be held liable when a minor child purchases necessities, based on the parents' legal obligation to care for the child.

The importance of the intra-family right to sue stems from the fact that the party held responsible must pay for medical or other treatment, usually by means of insurance or auto liability coverage. In such cases, suing your spouse or parent may be the only way to get the insurance company to pay up.

From 1950 to 1994, federal law required people who employed household workers — maids, nannies, babysitters, yard workers — to pay Social Security and Medicare taxes, if the worker's earnings exceeded $50 in three months or $200 a year. This meant in theory that an employer had to keep records, obtain IRS forms, deduct and pay taxes, and file forms every quarter, all under penalty of fines and/or jail time for failure to do so.

The law was widely ignored by household employers and employees who preferred cash and paying no taxes. The IRS estimated a 75% tax evasion rate. The hypocrisy of the situation became a national issue in 1993, when President Clinton nominated a lawyer to be U.S. attorney general, who, it was revealed, had failed to pay household employee taxes for years.

A second nominee had the same problem, as did a nominee for secretary of defense. One after another, the embarrassed nominees withdrew in a furor of press and public indignation known as "Nannygate."

Congress has since changed the law. The new law requires employers to withhold and pay taxes and report payments to household employees in excess of $1,000 annually on the employer's income tax return. Employees under 18 years of age listing their principal occupation as "student" are exempted from Social Security taxes. State income tax laws still apply to domestic workers, and many of these require quarterly filing. If in doubt, check with your accountant.

Name Changes

Technically, if you are no longer a minor, you can change your name without taking any legal action. Just start calling yourself by the new moniker and notify the people you think need to know about it.

But, in this day and age, such a free-spirited approach may cause you some problems. That is because you have an established Social Security number and account, bank accounts, a driver's license, credit cards and all the rest. The people who keep all those records are not going to look kindly on a mere phone call from you saying, "I just changed my name from John Smith to Joe Jones. Please change your records accordingly." Better to have your name changed officially, sanctioned by law.

Most states will require that you file a formal petition (obtained at the court house) requesting the name change and listing the old and new names. At the same time you file your petition, you must request a date for a court hearing on the petition, probably in four to six weeks. You may be required to tell all your creditors in writing, and even publish a notice in the local newspaper's classified legal notices for a few weeks, notifying the world about the hearing and your old and new names. Assuming no objections, the judge will grant your new name at the hearing. You can then obtain official copies of the decree declaring that you are now "Joe Jones" instead of "John Smith."

Some states issue official name change certificates, sort of like a "re-birth certificate," if you will. You will have to get a new U.S. passport, state driver's license, Social Security card and notify all those bureaucrats of your new status in life. By the time it is over, with court costs, newspaper ads and new official documents; it may cost you $200 to $300. If you use a lawyer, it will cost a lot more — at least double.

By custom, most women adopt their husband's surname at marriage, although there is no law requiring them to do so. Should a marriage end in divorce, upon request, the court will include in its decree a legal change of either party's married name.

Abortion

In 1973, the U.S. Supreme Court ruled that a pregnant woman has a right to abort her unborn child during the first six months of the pregnancy. Prior to this case, known as *Roe* v. *Wade*, most states had strict criminal and civil laws forbidding abortion. In the years since the 1973 ruling, abortion constantly has been a subject of court rulings and statutory actions by the states.

Although the basic right to an abortion remains, the Supreme Court has allowed the federal government and states to adopt three types of laws modifying this right to some degree: 1) laws requiring parental notification and/or consent before a minor can obtain an abortion, 2) restrictions on government funding of abortions, and 3) restrictions on abortion advertising.

As *Politico* reported in 2015: "Legislators have enacted scores of new laws in the past few years, from bans on most abortions after 20 weeks of pregnancy to requirements that doctors at abortion clinics have admitting privileges at a nearby hospital. Courts have blocked some measures and allowed others. And some statutes have taken effect without any pushback, typically in conservative regions where a federal appeals court would more likely support restrictions.

"The result is growing inconsistency nationally on the central legal argument of whether a state has created an "undue burden" for a woman seeking an abortion. That concept has guided the Supreme Court since the 1992 *Planned Parenthood* v. *Casey* decision, which upheld the right to abortion but granted states the power to regulate the procedure as long as excessive barriers — an undue burden — weren't created." Supporters of the right to life continue to advocate restrictions as safety measures, not abortion barriers, and that patient safety can't be considered an "undue burden."

Ownership of Animals

Pet ownership and care is a multi-billion dollar business in the U.S. According to the American Pet Products Association, Americans spent an all-time high of $55.7 billion on their pets in 2014 and spending in 2015 was estimated at close to $60 billion. It's no exaggeration to observe that many people are more concerned about the treatment of animals than about the fate of their fellow human beings.

If you purchase a pet from a store, the law presumes the animal to be in good health unless the seller states otherwise at the time of sale. If this turns out not to be true, the seller can be held liable for replacement or for reasonable veterinarian bills for treatment of the animal

There are many laws restricting animal ownership, including vaccination against rabies, annual licensing, zoning restrictions and lease and deed covenant restrictions specifying what kind of animal, if any, may be allowed in your home.

Occasionally, these fleecy, furry, and feathered friends can cause legal problems for their owners, their service industry, and those with whom they simply may have an unfortunate chance encounter. The long-standing, traditional rule governing household pets (like cats and dogs) is that their owners are not held responsible for human personal injury inflicted by them, unless the owner had prior knowledge of the animal's specific dangerous propensity to cause the injury.

However, many state or local laws now impose on pet owners strict liability for injury without regard to prior knowledge of a pet's peculiarities. Animals can also cause their owners to be held liable for property damage. Many local "leash laws" require animals to be kept on a leash when in public or enclosed in a secure place when at home. In any case, check your homeowner's insurance policy for your specific coverage.

An owner definitely is held responsible for injury caused by wild animals belonging to him or her, because of the "nature of the beast." If your pet ape or boa escapes and injures someone, you are just as liable as would be the San Diego Zoo in a similar situation. State laws permit the destruction of dangerous animals. But if the owner objects, an administrative or court hearing may be required before any final action can be taken against the animal.

The duty to protect and warn about wild animals in your care extends even to trespassers on your property. Of course if a burglar breaks into your house and is attacked by your Doberman watchdog that is usually accepted as reasonable force under the circumstances — just as if a human inflicted the damage.

What about the veterinarian? If your dog bites the doctor, that is usually an assumed risk on the vet's part — unless your animal is particularly nasty, in which case you must warn the vet. Most state laws give the vet a lien on your animal if you don't pay your bill, including boarding fees for the animal while the doctor awaits your payment. Just as in human medical treatment, an incompetent, reckless, or negligent veterinarian can be held liable for malpractice, but the obvious difficulty is in proving such charges.

Cruelty to Animals

Cruelty to animals is usually a state of local misdemeanor crime and includes failure to care for and feed the animal, or abandonment.

Under the federal "Animal Welfare Act of 1966," scientific researchers are required to avoid subjecting animals used in experiments to pain whenever possible, and to properly feed, house and care for them.

When an animal strays onto your property, you are allowed to use such reasonable force as may be necessary to remove it. In other words, you cannot use a gun when a broom would do. If some careless person kills your animal accidentally, you may recover the actual value of that animal. An AKC show dog might be worth $500 or more; a champion milk-producing Guernsey cow, thousands. If the person intentionally kills the animal without justification, you also may be able to recover punitive damages. Very few courts will allow damages for human emotional distress when a pet is killed.

CHAPTER 4:
BUSINESS AND EMPLOYMENT LAW

In this chapter, the three common ways of legally conducting business in the United States of America are discussed, with an emphasis on how well each system protects an individual from personal liability for potential business debts and claims. We also consider labor-management and employment law.

1. The Sole Proprietorship

One of the most common and least complicated ways to conduct business is for one to simply offer his or her services to the public as a single individual without any formal legal design. Such individuals are considered by the law to be *sole proprietors*, and are usually specialists in a craft or trade working by themselves, or with a few employees or independent contractors to assist them.

Usually, the operation is a small business enterprise — perhaps a secretarial service conducted from a person's home, a freelance writer, a yard and landscape service, or a house painting and small contracting operation.

There are no formal requirements for a person to become a sole proprietor. Just start working and do what is necessary to keep the business going and hopefully make a profit. However, the law forbids sole proprietors to represent themselves to the general public in a manner indicating they are either a corporation or partnership, each a legal status with defined rights upon which customers can rely.

Usually, a sole proprietor uses a business or trade name, but documents and bank accounts will state that it is "Jim Green, d.b.a. Green Lawn Service," for example. The "d.b.a." means "doing business as" and denotes a sole proprietorship. Most states have no registry of sole proprietorships, other than a roster of trade names used by such businesses. Once the "d.b.a." name is filed, it is protected from use by others. If you wish to establish a sole proprietorship, check with your state agency to see if there are any conflicts with your proposed name and existing trade names. A simple letter will get you on the list.

> **Comment:** *When I suggest throughout this text that you "check with a state agency" you should know that many states and their agencies have websites with plenty of useful information, including how to contact the agency via email, mail or phone.*

Unfortunately, both a sole proprietor and his or her property have no personal protection from business creditors or other claims. All the owner's personal assets are exposed to any business debts, and property used for the business can be attached by the owner's personal creditors. It is not unusual in this situation for personal and business cash accounts and property to be comingled, possibly endangering both. While business expenses are deductible, state and federal taxes are imposed on the business income as part of the personal earnings of the owner, and must be declared as such annually on that infamous IRS Form 1040.

The sole proprietorship may be a reasonable form to get started, but it is not recommended for any business owner seeking asset protection, or for those with increasing income and expanding sales or services.

While you certainly do not need a lawyer to form a sole proprietorship (you do it by your own actions), you may need one to help you with the eventual problems resulting from a business operation of this nature.

2. The Corporation

A *corporation* is an entity defined by the U.S. Supreme Court as "an artificial being, invisible, intangible, and existing only in contemplation of law." A more explicit definition is that a corporation is a legal "person" composed of one or more natural persons, entirely separate and distinct from the human individuals who compose it.

However abstract the corporation may be in theory, its recognition in law gives it great power. Much of business and trade in the United States is conducted in the corporate form, ranging in size from giants like Microsoft, General Motors and Exxon, down to your local "mom and pop" gas station/convenience stores.

There are at least five good reasons to incorporate your business or profession, including 1) to limit your personal liability, 2) to cut your tax bill, 3) to centralize management, 4) to permit uncomplicated transfer of interests and ownership, and 5) to make it easier to conduct business.

Most business and professional people are familiar with the term "limited liability." This refers to the fact that individuals who form a corporation to conduct business legally insulate themselves personally — and their real and personal property from any debts, lawsuits, and other claims which may arise against that business. The law holds the entity known as the "corporation" and its assets responsible for such claims, not the individuals who manage and own that corporation, the officers, the directors, and/or the shareholders.

Since corporations are entities "in contemplation of law," their formation, structure, and powers are governed by the laws of the 50 states, the District of Columbia and U.S. territories, such as Puerto Rico, Guam and the U.S. Virgin Islands. Corporation laws of the individual states still vary greatly. One state law says the duration of a corporation's legal existence is 25 years; in another, it is 99 years; in many, it is perpetual.

You can incorporate your company in any state, and the laws of that state will govern what you can and cannot do as a corporation. Some states have adopted laws and low taxes that are very corporate friendly. These states include Delaware, Wyoming and Nevada.

Incorporation Process

The term incorporation describes the process by which a corporation is formed under state law. You don't need an attorney to incorporate your business. In fact, the process is so simple that "do-it-yourself " incorporation kits, with documents tailored to the laws of each state, are available in most commercial stationery and business supply stores or on the Internet.

Both the purpose and name of your business must be included in the "articles of incorporation," a basic document you are required to file with the appropriate state agency, which varies in each state. Usually, registration will be with the office of the Secretary of State, the corporation counsel, the Department of Revenue, the Commerce Department, or a state agency with some similar title. The state agency will send you complete information about the incorporation process upon request, along with filing forms or it may be available on their website. Sometimes, a small fee is involved.

Once it is certain your proposed corporate name is not similar to or the same as an existing name, the *articles of incorporation* can be written and filed with the state. The articles should set out the names of the original incorporators (usually three persons are required), the purpose of the corporation, the directors' meeting requirements, the number and classes of shares authorized to be issued, the location of the office, name of the registered agent, and other major details.

(See sample on page 64.)

After the articles are filed and any initial corporate occupation taxes are paid, the corporate existence is a matter of public record — and you are ready to conduct business.

What kind of business activity needs the protection of a corporation?

The short answer is — any activity where you have a potential for liability. This is true if you have one or more employees; if you frequently interact with the public, clients, patients, or other businesses; if you are involved in joint ventures with others; if you engage in any hazardous activity; or, even if you just share space or facilities with other professionals with whom you are otherwise unassociated. If you are currently acting on your own in any of these business situations, unprotected as a sole proprietor, you could be just one lawsuit away from financial ruin.

More Reasons to Incorporate

Asset protection is not the only good reason for formation of a business corporation. You can also use a corporation to increase your available cash by paying minimal taxes and providing you with personal benefits.

Establishing the corporate form allows its officers and directors to have the company finance many expenses. For example, you can create a corporate health and medical expense reimbursement plan entirely paid for by the company, tax deductible as a business expense, with tax-free benefits to those included in the plan. The corporation can also pay for pension and other benefits for its officers. Other necessary expenditures that may be treated as legitimate business expenses include travel and the purchase of automobiles and equipment.

While the value of these goods and services have to be included in the recipient's gross income, these are tax-deductible business expenses for the corporation, which will reduce net income and, therefore, reduce company taxes. It is also less costly to include the value received in gross income rather than purchase the same things with your after-tax income.

In addition to health and pension benefits, tax breaks and limited liability, there are other solid reasons for incorporating:

- Ownership of shares of corporate stock is more easily transferable to family members as gifts or by sale to others (even by bequests at death), and transfers can be restricted in a closed corporation to a limited group, when working together is the objective.

- Since the corporation has a life of its own (in perpetuity), the death of officers or directors does not interrupt the business.

- Many businesses give corporate discounts for goods and services, such as air travel, which can add up to large savings.

Once the articles of incorporation are filed with the appropriate state agency, the corporate existence is a matter of public record, and you are ready to conduct business.

The one tax problem presented by the corporate form is *double taxation* — first, by imposition of the U.S. tax on corporate income, then by the personal income tax levied on dividends paid to shareholders, salaries, and other payments to officers and directors of the company. However, in an effort to promote small businesses, the federal government has provided some relief for this double taxation problem.

Once the articles of incorporation are filed with the appropriate state agency, the corporate existence is a matter of public record, and you are ready to conduct business.

Articles of Incorporation

ARTICLE I: The name of the corporation is _____

ARTICLE II: The mailing address of the corporation is _____ _____

ARTICLE III: The purpose of the corporation is_____ _____

ARTICLE IV: The aggregate number of authorized shares is _____

ARTICLE V: Cumulative voting of shares of stocks [*is*] [is *not*] authorized.

ARTICLE VI: Provisions limiting or denying to shareholders the preemptive right to acquire additional or treasury shares of the corporation are *(list limitations)*

_____

ARTICLE VII: Provisions for regulating the internal affairs of the corporation are_____*list*_____

ARTICLE VIII: The street address of the initial registered office of the corporation is _____and the name of the initial registered agent of the corporation at this address is ____*name*_____

ARTICLE IX: The address of the principal place of business is ____ _____ _____

ARTICLE X: The names and addresses of the persons who are to serve as directors until the first annual meeting of shareholders or until their successors are elected and shall qualify are:_____*list names*_____ _____ _____ _____

ARTICLE XI: The name and address of each incorporator is:

_____   _____

_____   _____

ARTICLE XII: The corporation shall indemnify any officer or director to the full extent permitted by law.

IN WITNESS WHEREOF, the undersigned incorporator has executed these Articles of Incorporation on this *date* day of *month*, 20_____

Incorporator's signature _____
Incorporator

Subchapter "S" Corporations

Subchapter "S" of the IRS tax code allows a small business corporation to elect to have the undistributed taxable income of the corporation taxed as personal income for the shareholders, thus avoiding payment of any corporate income tax.

Under the "S" election, if the company shareholders are your minor children, their combined reduced personal income status will mean still lower income taxes for everyone, adults included. Corporate losses can also be claimed directly by the shareholders. In this sense, the subchapter "S" tax status is like that of a general partnership, but it allows retaining the corporate liability protection that such a partnership does not enjoy.

A small business corporation can qualify for subchapter "S" treatment if it:

- is properly incorporated under state law
- has 35 or fewer shareholders
- has only one class of stock
- has shareholders who qualify as IRS-recognized individuals, estates, or trusts (other shareholding corporations or partnerships do not qualify) and;
- is not "affiliated" with another corporation (meaning it does not hold 80 percent or more ownership of another corporation).

Corporate Structure

Corporations have the advantage of a defined centralized management structure with consolidated control, flexibility, and permanency — and limited liability for shareholders. Corporate powers are so all-inclusive that they are almost co-extensive with the powers a human individual can exercise in business.

Most state laws minimally require this basic corporate structure: The owners of a corporation are the shareholders who own stock in the company; the board of directors manages the business; and the officers (president, vice president, secretary, and treasurer) are responsible for day-to-day operations.

Be aware that if state law allows, small corporations can operate with only one or two stockholders, directors, and officers (several or all of whom may be the same person). Many states, like Delaware, New York and Nevada, allow one-person corporations. This minimum requirement for only one director satisfies what sounds like complicated requirements of state law (mostly "paperwork") and makes a company relatively easy to run.

A stock corporation is one which issues capital stock divided into shares held by the owners of the corporation, known as shareholders, and which is authorized by law to pay its profits to the shareholders in the form of dividends. Generally, stock corporations, shares of which are not listed or traded on a stock exchange, are known as privately owned companies and are usually exempt from federal laws controlling the issuance and registration of securities.

Organization & Operation

Once the state officially recognizes your corporation, the first step is to hold an organizational meeting to elect the board of directors and officers, adopt bylaws, price initial stock values, approve contracts of employment, and authorize other start-up procedures, such as opening a company bank account.

The board will be required to meet at least once a year for the election of officers and directors and other business. Full and accurate minutes of all meetings must be kept — both to satisfy the law and protect the corporate status. Like other legal entities, corporations have the power to hold title to property, enter into contracts, sue and be sued and to do all things necessary for its business. Corporations exist in perpetuity or until they are dissolved either by the directors or by the state — the latter usually occurs after failure to pay annual operating fees or taxes, or failure to file required reports.

Since your company is likely to be a closely held corporation, it is important to make it clear to the general public and to creditors that they are dealing with a corporation — not you personally. Failure to make known the use of the corporate business form can result in a loss of limited liability protection for individual officers and directors, negating the whole purpose of incorporating. Most state laws require your company name to include words notifying the public of your corporate form, such as "Inc." (incorporated), "Corp." (corporation), "Ltd." (limited), or "Co." (company).

Use of corporate checking accounts, stationery, business cards, and documents (always signed in a corporate capacity) will protect you and the company — and allow people to easily understand that they are doing business with a corporation, not an individual acting under a trade or company name.

Maintaining the corporate identity is especially important when obtaining financing for a new business, which will often require personal guarantees for loans, unless the corporation is well-capitalized. All loan documents should clearly reflect whether it is the corporation or the individual who is primarily responsible for repayment. Officers should always indicate their official company position when signing on its behalf, following their name with their corporate title or adding a phrase such as "for the XYZ Co., Inc."

Officers, directors, and controlling shareholders have a general fiduciary duty of loyalty and care which should govern all their corporate conduct. (A *fiduciary* is a person to whom property or power is entrusted for the benefit of others.) Unless they breach that duty by gross negligence or by acting in bad faith, they usually will have no liability to third parties. Third parties have to prove personal wrongful conduct on the part of a company official or director in order to hold them responsible for actions which would support application of the legal doctrine known as *piercing the corporate veil.*

Piercing the Corporate Veil

There are possible breaches in the wall of personal liability provided by incorporation, and, for your asset safety, you should know how these exceptions come about.

Certain acts of directors and officers may be grounds for a company creditor to ask a court to "pierce the corporate veil," which means just what it says. For example, if the corporation cannot pay a creditor's proven debt or a judgment claim, the individuals behind the corporation can be held personally responsible for its obligations, even though they have given no personal guarantees. This can happen when:

- Corporate debt is knowingly incurred when the company is already insolvent

- Required annual shareholders or board of directors meetings are not held, or other corporate formalities are not observed

- Corporate records, especially minutes of directors meetings, are not properly or adequately maintained

- Shareholders remove unreasonable amounts of funds from the corporation, endangering its financial stability

- There is a pattern of consistent non-payment of dividends, or payment of excessive dividends
- There is a general comingling of actions or funds of the corporation, and those belonging personally to the person or persons who control the corporation; or
- There is a failure to maintain separate offices, or the company has little other business and is used only as a façade for the activities of the dominant shareholder.

In order to maintain personal limited liability, it is essential these described actions be avoided. In recent years, courts have delighted in finding new excuses for holding directors, officials and shareholders liable for corporate liabilities.

Other activities which courts have found to be the basis for personal liability have included improper corporate guarantees of loans or contracts benefiting an officer, timing of the sale of a controlling interest for self-benefit, profiting from inside information, transactions with other businesses which can be held to be conflicts of interest, unreasonable loans to company officials, and extension of unwarranted credit.

Directors are generally held to a higher standard of duty than officers because they hold the ultimate controlling power, including the election or removal of officers.

THE CASE OF THE DIRECTOR'S DECEIT

Peter Davis was president, a director and principal shareholder of Davis Investments Inc., an apparently successful stock brokerage firm. Using the company's name and credit, Davis ran up large expenses for personal activity, including entertainment, travel, and purchases of luxury items. He also withdrew large sums from company bank accounts to pay personal gambling debts. Davis knew the company was short of cash and deeply in debt.

When this corporate house of cards collapsed, both Davis Inc. and Mr. Davis were sued by creditors who found no assets left to pay the corporate debts. Based on these facts, a court held Mr. Davis to be personally liable for the debt, ruling the company was little more than a fraudulent shell device used to deceive creditors. The creditors took his home, office, personal property and bank accounts. Davis' corporate veil was thoroughly pierced.

Without any need for the IRS to "pierce the corporate veil," directors and officers can also be held liable for federal taxes owed by the corporation — both corporate income tax on the annual business net profit and for unpaid payroll taxes for employees.

As an extra asset protection arrangement, experts recommend that in a closely held family corporation, only one spouse serve as a director — thus limiting potential family liability in the event the corporate veil is pierced by adverse legal action. One-spouse operations are easily possible in states where one-person corporations are permitted, like Delaware, Wyoming or Nevada.

State of Incorporation

The state in which you live, or in which you intend to do business, is usually the best state in which to incorporate. Any business which incorporates in one state and does business in another, will be required to "qualify to do business" in that other state. This means formally registering, paying a franchise tax or other initial tax, filing annual reports and paying annual taxes in the second state — all because your corporation is a "foreign corporation," chartered in another state.

In other words, the red tape is doubled by incorporation in one state, and doing business in another. If you have a multi-state business operation, this is an acceptable burden, but if not, this places a premium on incorporating in the state in which you are located and doing business.

Limited Liability Corporations

All 50 states and the District of Columbia have adopted laws allowing the creation of the limited liability corporation (LLC), a hybrid mix of the best features of both a close corporation and a partnership. LLCs are designed to avoid restrictions while taking advantage of the tax benefits of a subchapter "S" corporation.

The LLC combines into one legal entity the elements of an unincorporated association with the corporation's separate existence from its owners and their limited liability. But, as in a partnership (see below), the LLC can be created and operated according to an agreement by or among its owners, without having to adhere to the corporate formalities. It can also serve as a pass through non-taxable entity so that, as with a partnership, all tax effects and consequences are those of the members alone.

Most states now allow single-person LLCs, but some require two or more members. Since an LLC can serve for any legal business purpose, it has become suddenly popular with accountants, and has spread to doctors' offices, real estate ventures, and garden variety "mom and pop" enterprises.

The LLC's chief advantage is the personal liability protection it affords to its members, especially in a time when people sue at the drop of a hat. Many existing close corporations and partnerships have begun converting their legal structure to the LLC format Since the LLC is relatively new, check with a business law attorney if you want more details.

3. Partnerships

Forming a general or limited partnership, particularly a "family partnership" — one of the best-known variations — can greatly reduce federal and state income and inheritance taxes and provide maximum personal insulation from lawsuits and other potential liabilities.

Used successfully in the United States for almost two centuries, the continuing popularity of the limited partnership among knowledgeable financial planners attests to its effectiveness in protecting assets — but only if properly organized and operated as the law requires.

General Partnerships

In the broadest sense, a general partnership is an association of two or more persons (or other legal entities) formed to conduct a business for mutual profit. More than 90% of all partnerships in the United States are general partnerships governed by the "1997 Uniform Partnership Act," that is now law in 35 states. The remaining states adopted an earlier version of the law and Louisiana has its own specialized statute.

In a general partnership, each partner is a co-owner, jointly running the business with the objective of making a profit, each partner acting as agents for, and having a fiduciary relationship with one another. As a result, each partner is personally liable for the acts of the others, including partnership debts and liabilities. In a general partnership, by their common agreement, the partners may have the same or differing capital investments and may share profits and losses in the same or varying proportions, usually corresponding to each partner's original investment.

A partnership is recognized by the law for purposes such as making contracts, obtaining credit, filing bankruptcy, incurring debt, marshalling assets and acquiring and transferring property. But a partnership, as such, does not pay tax — its partners do — as individuals owing income tax on their partnership income.

A general partnership can present some major liability problems.

For instance, each general partner can be held personally liable for all partnership debts and liabilities resulting from another partner's or an agent's negligent or harmful acts. A general partnership often must be dissolved when one partner files personal bankruptcy or dies, unless immediate arrangements are made for a buyout of that partner's interest, or unless the partnership agreement anticipates such events and makes contingent continuation provisions. Usually, a deceased general partner's interest is subjected to estate probate often a lengthy and cumbersome process — and estate and inheritance taxes are levied on the value of that interest, diminishing what goes to the heirs.

Limited Partnerships

A limited partnership must be composed of at least one general partner (who is usually the managing partner) and one or more "limited partners" (sometimes called "special partners").

The limited partner, who must take no part in the day-to-day management, has no personal liability beyond the amount of his or her agreed amount of cash or other capital investment in the partnership. The limited partner does have a right to receive agreed amounts of partnership income when it is distributed. This arrangement is accomplished by specific written provisions in the partnership agreement, the basic document governing the partnership to which all partners are parties.

The 1916 and 1976 versions of the Uniform Limited Partnership Act were adopted in 49 states, the District of Columbia, and the U.S. Virgin Islands. The revised 2001 Act has been adopted in 17 states. These acts set the rights and responsibilities of the limited and general partners among themselves, and with other people with whom they have business dealings. The major features of this law are as follows: protecting the limited partner from liability as a general partner (unless he or she actually takes an active part in control of the business); giving the limited partner full rights and access to all partnership information; and guaranteeing the limited partner his or her share of the profits or other compensation by way of regular income payments.

Perhaps one of the greatest advantages afforded by a limited partnership is that a personal creditor of a limited partner usually cannot attach that partner's interest in the partnership.

Such a personal creditor can only obtain what is known as a "charging order," a relatively unattractive remedy in the judgment collection process, usually requiring the creditor to wait for some future distribution of partnership income to the debtor partner. However, future distributions are a totally discretionary act within the power of the managing partner. In other words, a creditor could wait forever.

The Uniform Limited Partnership Act establishes the general procedure, and many state statutes require a formal procedure for formation and registration of a limited partnership. As notice and protection to the public, the law often requires the formal public registration of partnership agreements; the filing of a "certificate of affirmation," or a formal articles of a limited partnership signed and registered with a state agency or with the county clerk as notice of the business' scope and the limits of each partner's liability.

Usually, the law forbids the public use of the name of a limited partner as part of the partnership name (unless it is the same family name of the managing or other general partner). This is so that a false reliance will not be created in the mind of the public concerning that limited partner's liability. It is a basic legal requirement that, in order to preserve his or her limited liability, a limited partner cannot take any active role in the actual management of the partnership.

The rules of law applicable to the formation of contracts also generally apply to a partnership agreement. There must be valid consideration (something of value must be paid or pledged), individual legal capacity to enter into a contract, and informed consent. But the essential distinguishing feature of a partnership is that it is an agreement to conduct a joint business for the mutual profit of the partners.

The Uniform Limited Partnership Act requires there be at least one general partner who actually manages the business. This general partner, by the terms of the agreement, may be given complete or shared management control with another general partner, but each general partner is also fully personally liable as such for the partnership debts and liabilities. It is not uncommon for the general partner to be empowered to make decisions about the needs for additional working capital to expand the business, or whether or not profits are to be withheld from limited partners and used instead for future development.

The success of a limited partnership depends greatly on the management abilities of the person who serves as general partner. Therefore, agreements often provide that the partnership will dissolve (unless all the partners agree to its continuation) upon a general partner's death, bankruptcy, transfer of his or her interest while still alive, or legal incompetency. For a general managing partner, even one who holds a small portion (say five percent) of the partnership assets, his or her status confers near total control over the entire business enterprise — which may be worth many millions of dollars. At the time of the general managing partner's death, however, estate inheritance taxes will be levied only on the value of his or her small interest.

Thus, a person who serves as a general partner, with his or her spouse and heirs as limited partners, can limit his or her estate and inheritance taxes.

A general partner does share in all profits, and since partnerships are not taxed as such, he or she can avoid the double taxation imposed on corporations (the tax on corporate profits, plus individual income taxes on corporate officers' salaries and shareholders' dividends). General partners have the ability to withdraw their full contributions without taxation, and general partners jointly manage and conduct the business with complete access to all books and financial information, and can obtain joint credit with other partners.

If it is done right, the family limited partnership is good for:
- income-shifting device
- conducting a family business where the corporate form presents tax problems

The Managing General Partner

Family Partnership

- maintaining control of assets while passing them on to others
- estate planning
- insulation from creditor attacks

The legal relationship popularly known as a family partnership usually is created as a vehicle to transfer income and assets from:

1. The owner/organizer of a business

2. Anyone who accumulates valuable assets or

3. Anyone who is in a high income tax bracket to members of his or her own family in order to limit everyone's personal and tax liability to the maximum extent possible

A family partnership is really nothing more than a limited partnership in which family members, rather than non-family business associates, are the limited partners. A parent or grandparent is usually the managing general partner.

In contrast to a family "corporation," which many use to protect assets, a family limited partnership includes an agreement allowing the parties great precision in defining their rights, withdrawal of property with far fewer tax problems and it has no stockholder restrictions.

In order to protect a family limited partnership from possible legal challenges, there should be a formal written agreement that spells out the limits and powers of each partner, and a complete record of all filings and transactions. The managing partner should be paid reasonable compensation, and transfers to the donee partners (especially minors) should not be in the form of discharging normal parental obligations like medical care and educational support. Trustees for minors should be completely independent, and thus not in any way subject to the donee's control. Title to assets should be formally transferred to the family partnership so that it becomes the true owner of record.

In order to recognize a minor child as a limited partner, courts will almost always require the appointment of a fiduciary trustee with complete powers to manage the minor's interest. The only exception occurs in the exceedingly rare instance when a minor has sufficient maturity and ability to act on his or her own as a limited partner.

Family partnerships have several advantages:

- These arrangements are simple in form, needing only an agreement, a deed of gift, and a certificate of family limited partnership. Property need be transferred only once to the partnership and later changes of donor and done interests require only amendments to the partnership documents. The only public records involved are deeds to real estate transfers and registration of the partnership itself if state law requires this, although most states do.

- Deeding real property to the partnership eliminates the need at the time the donor dies for ancillary probates of property located in states other than that of the donee's residence. Most states exempt such partnership property from probate.

- The donor of property transfers title but still retains a great measure of personal control over the property, especially when he or she is the managing general partner.

- Since a partnership is not a taxable entity, making gifts through the medium of a family partnership avoids the double taxation to which net income is subjected in an ordinary family corporation.

THE CASE OF THE PUMPKIN PATCH PARTNERSHIP

Jake Jackson, a 55-year-old widower, is concerned about the economic future of his adult daughters, Mary Jo, Sue Ellen, and Norma Jean. Jake personally owns a successful pumpkin farm and produce business, valued in the millions.

To alleviate his worries, Jake and his daughters — all of whom work in the business — form a family limited partnership, with Jake as managing general partner owning 5% of the partnership assets. The remaining 95% interest is divided equally among the girls as limited partners.

Jake deeds his produce business and pumpkin farm to the partnership. Under the partnership agreement, Jake is paid an appropriate salary for the remainder of his life. He controls the business and property, and upon his death, the limited partners can choose his successor and equally inherit his interest. During his lifetime, several of Jake's grandchildren are also made limited partners, with appropriate shares of interest coming from their own mother's share by mutual agreement.

Jake avoids personal income taxes except on his actual partnership salary and dividends, and the arrangement divides income (and tax liabilities) amongst its limited partners, reducing total taxes substantially. When Jake dies, only 5% interest is subject to probate and estate tax.

For the Jacksons, a family limited partnership is a good income shifting device. It avoids taxes on a family business the corporate form would impose and allows Jake to control assets while passing them on to his heirs. It also helps estate planning, and provides insulation from creditor attacks.

Legally speaking and tax-wise, the Jacksons are one big happy family of partners.

The Limited Partner

In order for a limited partner to effect and maintain his or her limited liability: 1) the limited partnership must be created in good faith compliance with all statutes; 2) a limited partner's surname cannot be used in the business; 3) no false statements, known to a limited partner and on which third parties rely, can be made on the registration form; and 4) a limited partner can take no part in the conduct of the business.

A limited partner cannot assign, sell, or mortgage his or her interest in any specific partnership property, because to do so would be to destroy the voluntary nature of the partnership association — in effect forcing a new partner on the others without their consent. But a limited partner can assign, sell, or mortgage his or her property interest to another partner, assuming the articles of partnership do not forbid this.

A limited partner's interest in specific partnership property (title to which he or she holds jointly with the other partners in what the law calls a tenancy in partnership) cannot be subjected to garnishment, attachment, or execution by a personal judgment creditor of that partner. First claim on partnership assets rests with creditors of the partnership itself.

From the foregoing, you can properly conclude that a family limited partnership has great potential as a shelter from creditors for both personal and family business assets and certainly it can help to reduce estate and inheritance taxes. Income taxes can also be reduced substantially as family partnership income is spread among all partner/family members, including younger members with less income, meaning a lower overall family income tax rate.

But limited partnerships, family-based or otherwise, come at a price.

You must be exceedingly careful in complying with all local and state laws and regulations governing registration, firm names and the use of fictitious business names. Separate partnership bank accounts must be established with legal control of the funds clearly indicated.

If a donee is to be a limited partner, his or her partnership interest must be reflected in all insurance policies, deeds, leases, business contracts and in any litigation that may occur.

All statutory documentary requirements must be scrupulously met, and complete financial records maintained on an annual basis. Tax returns must be filed. Most importantly, when donor interests are involved, the donor must fully transfer to the donee all rights, titles and interest in order to avoid tax or legal contests of the partnership status.

While there is flexibility in a family partnership, especially for the managing general partner, there are also restrictions. The donor of the partnership assets still must deed absolutely his or her assets to the partnership and normally all of the partners must agree before partnership assets can be sold or transferred. As with any partnership, unless the partnership agreement specifically provides otherwise, one partner's death or bankruptcy may force the dissolution of the partnership (or a forced buyout) at an inopportune time for the sale and distribution of assets.

Unless carefully crafted by experienced legal experts, your partnership may be vulnerable to IRS officials or creditors eager to use legal loopholes to destroy your protection. That could mean that after you are gone, and well after creating an ostensible family partnership, your family may find itself in a financial and asset situation far worse than if nothing had been done.

But since this form of asset ownership and business has been around for 200 years — the problems (and the way around them) are well known and can be avoided. There are no "short cuts" per se, but there are many possible rewards.

Chapter 4

4. Labor-Management and Employment Law

You do not have to be a student of American history to know this nation has a long record of contentious, and sometimes violent, disputes between labor and management. From the post-Civil War era when industrialization began, right up through the Great Depression (1929-1941), many U.S. business leaders viewed workers' demands for better pay, a 40-hour work week, safer work places and prohibition of child labor as pure socialism — if not Communism.

Although labor violence is rare now, labor and management have long since realized their common stake in working out their differences peacefully. Now they argue over health insurance coverage, seniority work rules, profit sharing and overtime pay.

This reasonableness has been produced, in part, by economic necessity but also by federal laws, which govern most labor relations, first recognizing workers' rights and then balancing those with management's rights. The general authority of the federal government in this area is based on the Article I constitutional power to regulate interstate commerce.

In the early 1930s, the Norris-LaGuardia Act removed the power of courts to issue injunctions against almost all forms of workers' strikes — a favorite management tactic in the old days. It also outlawed contracts forcing workers to agree not to join a union. The National Labor Relations ("Wagner") Act of 1935 guaranteed workers the right to organize and join a union, to bargain collectively, and forbid management from interfering with these rights. It established the National Labor Relations Board (NLRB) to enforce the new law.

The 1947 Taft-Hartley Act moved in the direction of management, banning closed union shops, defining unfair labor practices by unions, and setting up procedures to halt strikes that endanger national safety. The 1954 Landrum-Griffin Labor Reform Act curbed the influence of corruption in unions, gave union members a protected "bill of rights" against corrupt union officials, and banned union boycotts or strikes aimed at specific products or used to force collective bargaining with certain unions.

Under the Wagner Act, an employee is any person earning wages, salaries, or commissions, not including farm workers, domestic servants, people working for their spouse or parent, railroad employees (who are covered by their own law) and independent contractors. An independent contractor is different from an employee in that the worker controls his or her own work methods, being accountable to management only for the final product. Temporary workers, a more recent but very important labor phenomenon, are independent contractors in relation to the places they are assigned to work, although they may be employees of the "temp" company, depending on the terms of their contract.

This distinction is important because the status of a worker defines his or her rights and remedies in various situations. For example, an employee is covered by workman's compensation laws; an independent contractor is not. Also, an independent contractor is responsible for filing and paying his or her own taxes, whereas the employer must do this for an employee. The IRS considers certain professionals (like doctors, lawyers, engineers, accountants, consultants, real estate agents, carpenters, and plumbers) to be independent contractors, while most other workers are presumed to be employees. In some states, such as Florida, the law allows an employer an absolute right to dismiss an employee without giving any cause. In other states causes must be stated.

Federal, state and local government employees now have the right to organize in unions and bargain for rights, but they do not have the right to strike — a point dramatically made in 1981 when President Ronald Reagan fired more than 11,000 striking air traffic controllers employed by the Federal Aviation Agency. Indeed, Massachusetts Governor Calvin Coolidge's famous response to the Boston police strike of 1919 gave him national recognition that led to his nomination for vice president, in which he said, "There is no right to strike against the public safety by anybody, anywhere, anytime."

Certain other federal laws establish a minimum hourly wage for certain classes of workers and require safe working conditions, such as the Occupational Safety and Health Act of 1970.

Discrimination in Employment

The Civil Rights Act of 1964, particularly Title 7, and the Equal Employment Opportunity Act of 1974 guarantee to all workers in businesses of 15 or more employees the right not to be discriminated against based on race, religion, color, sex, or national origin. These rights include hiring, promotion, and equal pay for equal work. There are a few instances in which discrimination can be legal in employment, as when only women are hired as attendants for ladies' restrooms.

An employee or prospective employee claiming discrimination must prove he or she had the qualifications for the job, and that persons not of their race, religion, color, sex, or national origin were hired (or not fired) for the same job in other words, that he or she was treated differently only because of such personal characteristics.

The Age Discrimination in Employment Act of 1967 makes it illegal for firms of 20 or more employees to discriminate against a person between the ages of 40 and 70 years old. Employees also have a right to be free from sexual harassment in the workplace, and those subjected to such treatment can sue for damages. Sexual harassment is defined as unwelcomed sexual advances and offensive or obscene remarks that make working conditions uncomfortable or intolerable, or create hostility or intimidation.

Complaints regarding all of these possible instances of employment discrimination can be filed by an injured party with the U.S. Equal Employment Opportunities Commission (EEOC) or a similar state agency, or a suit can be filed in the appropriate court. The EEOC complaint form is a one-page document that is easy to fill out. But the EEOC is so understaffed, it may take years for your complaint to be heard and decided. The EEOC does have the power to order a worker's hiring, reinstatement or promotion, award back pay, and order an end to an employer's discriminatory practices. Since 1993, the number of EEOC cases has soared from 11,908 to nearly 89,000 in 2014.

The 1990 Americans with Disabilities Act (ADA) forbids discrimination in employment or access to public services based on mental or physical disabilities. Taking effect in July 1992, the Act forbids such discrimination in employment, receipt of public services and participation in public programs, and access to places of business and telecommunications facilities. Reasonable accommodations for disabled people must be made by federal and state agencies and by private businesses with 15 or more employees.

Another addition to the legal rights of employees is the Family Medical Leave Act of 1993, requiring employers to grant a reasonable amount of unpaid leave when an employee or members of his or her family are ill or pregnant. Lilly Ledbetter Fair Pay Act of 2009 extended the time during which an employee can file equal pay discrimination complaints.

> **Comment:** *In most cases when a dispute or problem with an employer arises, an employee's last resort should be a lawyer. Employers, like everyone else, want to avoid litigation. Try a private discussion with your supervisor or boss, then mediation or arbitration as the next best route. Be informed about your rights, get the details right, and arm yourself with good documentation. Control your emotions and stick to the facts. Talking about your complaint with fellow employees can only further undermine your position with management. Advice concerning wages, hours, and overtime is available from the nearest office of the U.S. Department of Labor or your state's equivalent agency. Check the government web site for listings.*

Other Rights & Obligations

When an employee creates an invention that can be patented or material that can be copyrighted, his or her employment contract will determine whether these are the property of the employer or the employee. Work contracts usually give such rights to the employer. When an employer commissions a writer to produce a book or article for a magazine, it may be stated that it is a work for hire arrangement, in which case the employer owns the copyrighted work.

If you leave one job for another, a general rule of law prevents you from using or divulging any confidential information belonging to your former employer. That employer can sue to protect trade secrets and recover damages if proven. Usually, disputes about confidential information arise over an ex-employee's use of customer lists, which may or may not actually be "confidential" in the sense that such names are often readily available from other sources.

The law recognizes the validity of, and courts will enforce, a reasonable contract not to compete, in which one party agrees not to compete in business with the other party. This kind of restriction can cover an employee after leaving his or her job — you don't want your cordon bleu French chef quitting mid-contract to work next door at another restaurant — but, more often, it arises when one person buys an existing business from another. You don't want Stanley to establish another barber shop across the street from the one you just bought from him.

Courts will not enforce such provisions if they are unreasonable in time duration or geographic area. No competition for one year in the same town or county is likely to be found acceptable by a court, but not a guarantee to never to work again in the United States in a similar business.

Some labor-management agreements and employment contracts require both parties in certain defined circumstances to submit disputes to arbitration — the hearing and determination of a controversy by a neutral person given power to make a decision, called an "award," that settles the issue. This differs from mediation, which is when a person or panel of experts tries to bring the parties of a dispute together in a common agreement.

Customers who have disputes with banks or credit card companies often can be forced to go to arbitration before a private lawyer to try to resolve the problem, rather than before a judge in court. That's because many financial accounts come with built-in contracts containing "pre-dispute" arbitration clauses, so-named because consumers agree to them when they sign up for the account, before they actually have a disagreement. If you open an account, check to see what your dispute rights are before you sign.

Many people believe arbitration is useful because it moves far more quickly than the courts with their large backlog of civil cases, and its procedure is streamlined. Many states have a uniform arbitration statute, and courts will cooperate in various ways to ratify arbitration awards, which are equivalent to a judicial judgment in many respects.

Contract Not to Compete

FOR GOOD CONSIDERATION, the undersigned agrees not to compete with the business of *name of company* and its lawful successors and assigns.

The undersigned shall not directly or indirectly engage in a business or other activity described as:_____

_____

_____

_____

notwithstanding whether said participation be as an owner, officer, director, employee, agent, consultant, or partner.

This covenant shall extend only for a radius of *number* miles from the present location of the *name*_____ Company located at *address of company* and shall remain in full force and effect for *number* years from the date hereof.

In the event of any breach, the Company shall be entitled to full injunctive relief without need to post bond, which rights shall be cumulative with and not necessarily successive or exclusive of any other legal rights.

This contract shall be binding upon and inure to the benefit of the parties, their successors, assigns, and personal representatives.

Signed this *date* day of *month*, 20___.

In the presence of:

*Witness's signature*_____ *First party's signature*_____
Witness   First Party

*Witness's signature*_____ *Second party's signature*_____
Witness   Second Party

The law recognizes the validity of (and the courts will enforce) a reasonable contract not to compete, in which one party agrees not to compete in business with the other party.

Agency

Agency is a relationship between two or more persons by which one (the principal) gives another (the agent) the right to act in his or her behalf in such a way as to legally bind the principal. This area of the law is considerable in extent, but most often arises in a business or employment context. A form of agency occurs when an employer (the master) authorizes an employee (the servant) to act on his behalf during the course of his employment. There are several means of creating and terminating an agent's status, and agency issues usually arise when there are subsequent disputes over whether in fact a person was an agent, and if so, what the scope of his or her authority was in a given situation so as to bind the principal by his acts.

What About Retirement?

Many employers have pension plans covering qualified employees who work for the company for a minimum period of years and contribute to the retirement fund. The employer usually matches the worker's contribution. Most plans allow the retiring employee to elect either to receive pension payments, or take out a "lump sum" of accumulated cash from the fund that can be re-invested in other financial options like individual retirement accounts (IRAs), 401(k) or Roth or Keogh plans, all IRS-recognized private retirement alternatives.

One very important factor to weigh before choosing a monthly pension payment plan is the financial soundness of your employer. Many U.S. companies have long skimped on employee pension fund contributions producing a large gap between promised employee benefits and real assets needed to pay retired workers. More than 65,000 pension plans in theory are covered by federal insurance, but no one pretends a general pension collapse could be paid for by the government.

The Pension Benefit Guarantee Corporation an official U.S. government agency that "insures" pension plans calculates that the combined shortfall in these plans was about $500 billion in 2014. That's the difference between assets on hand and obligations. It raises the question: Who will insure the insurer? Meanwhile, many companies have eliminated private pensions altogether. General Motors alone admits to $24 billion in unfunded pension liability.

In 2014, state public pension plans were underfunded by $4.7 trillion, up from $4.1 trillion in 2013. Overall, the combined state plans' funded status was only 36%. Estimates added $400 billion of unfunded liabilities at the large-city level.

For people with the sophistication to choose careful investments, the safest course may be to take the lump sum and invest it elsewhere. As long as pension money is transferred directly ("rolled over") into an individual retirement account (IRA), it escapes the 20% withholding tax imposed on straight pension withdrawals. If you need money later, you can cash in some of your new investments, paying ordinary income tax rates (the top marginal rate is now 39.6%) on only the amount withdrawn.

Many people find it a nightmare to choose the right investments guaranteeing a retirement income. They don't want to be their own pension manager and actuarial expert. The alternative may be the purchase of an annuity that guarantees payment over a set period of years or for life.

Many company pension plans, so-called section "401(k)" accounts, and profit sharing plans allow the choice of an annuity at retirement. Direct transfers of such funds can be made by your company to the insurance company issuing the annuity, thus avoiding the 20% tax.

Be careful: The amount paid back in life income per $1,000 invested in domestic U.S. annuities will vary widely among insurance companies. Often, a higher yield can be a sign of a higher-risk company. Prices vary because companies use different mortality assumptions and have different management expenses. This means that careful annuity shopping can produce 20–25% more in life income if you have the time and expertise to find the right company.

Given the lax, contradictory state regulatory policies governing American insurance companies and a record of multiple insurer failures, it makes sense to look for safety if an annuity is your retirement choice. A possible alternative: Some of the soundest and best run insurers issuing annuities are in Switzerland. Any good investment advisor can give you names and locations.

For detailed advice, consult a reputable financial advisor. But for the lowest costs and highest yields in retirement income, make plans while you are relatively young.

CHAPTER 5:
WILLS, TRUSTS AND GUARDIANSHIPS

In this chapter, we review the basic legal methods available to a person to direct the distribution of his or her property after death, the creation and financing of mechanisms to care for others both during life and after death, and prearranged techniques that can provide supervision for those legally unable to care for themselves.

1. Wills

A last will and testament is a written document in which a person (if male — *testator*; if female — the *testatrix*) directs the exact manner in which he or she wishes to have his or her property (known as the estate) distributed or disposed of, effective after his or her death. A will may also address the issue of a guardian for a person's minor children.

A gift of real property in a will is called a *devise*, and the person receiving it is the *devisee*. A gift of personal property is a *legacy* or *bequest*, and the recipient is the *legatee*.

A person who dies without making a will is said to die *intestate*, in which case the person's property is distributed to family members and next of kin according to the laws of intestacy effective in the state where the deceased was a resident. These laws vary greatly from one state to another and often do not mirror the actual wishes of the deceased, which is one of many good reasons why everyone should create a will.

A valid will may be made by any person who has reached the age of majority (18 years) and is of "sound mind." To be valid, a will must: 1) be in writing, 2) meet the statutory requirements imposed in the state of residence, 3) be intended by its maker as a will, 4) dispose of property after death, and 5) be revocable during the maker's lifetime.

The form is not as important as the intention in the making of a will, but state laws do impose basic requirements. For a valid will, most state statutes require these formalities: 1) a signature by the testator, or the use of a mark such as an "X," either of which can be placed anywhere on the document in some states, but in others must be placed only at the end; 2) two or three disinterested non-beneficiary witnesses of the testator's signature (the number depending on the state) who also sign the will; and 3) an official notarization in some states. (See sample on next page.)

There are various types of wills. A holographic will is one the testator writes out, dates and signs in his or her own handwriting and is recognized as valid in about half the states, usually requiring no witnesses. There are also joint, mutual and reciprocal wills in which two or more persons execute wills at the same time with common objectives.

Here is something to remember: The law does not favor disinheriting a spouse or child. If a will is silent on this subject, and no specific provision is made for them, probate courts will presume it was an oversight and grant the next of kin his or her statutory share of your estate. If you really mean to exclude a spouse or child from inheritance, you must specifically indicate the exclusion in your will.

Validity & Revocation

A will may be declared invalid if it can be proven to have been the result of fraud or an undue influence on the testator, or if the testator is mentally incompetent or under the age of majority.

A will may be revoked by a mentally competent testator at any time prior to death by: 1) executing a new and later will; 2) by any written document clearly revoking the prior will; or 3) by a testator's personally destroying the will or directing another person to do so.

A will should be periodically reviewed by the testator, because circumstances constantly change in life. If a testator chooses to change the terms of an original will, revoke part of it, or add new provisions, this is done by executing a codicil, an official document specifying the desired modifications. This instrument requires all the formalities of the original will. If changes are extensive, it is best to write a new will, in which the first one is formally revoked by reference.

Last Will and Testament

I, *your full Legal name*, a resident of the County of *your county*, in the State of *your state*, being of sound mind and under no duress, do hereby make and declare this to be my Last Will and Testament, and do hereby revoke and cancel all previous wills and codicils at any time made by me.

ARTICLE I. I am married to *spouse's name*, and all references to "my spouse" in this document are to *spouse's name*. My children now living are *names of children*   .

ARTICLE II. I appoint *executor's name* as Executor of this, my Last Will and Testament, to serve without bond. If my Executor is unable or unwilling to serve, then I appoint *alternate executor's name* as alternate Executor, also to serve without bond.

ARTICLE III. I hereby direct my Executor to pay all of my legal debts, obligations and funeral expenses from my estate as an expense of administration, without reimbursement from any person. I also authorize my Executor to settle, compromise, and discharge any claims against my estate in his or her absolute discretion.

ARTICLE IV. I hereby give and bequeath my entire estate to my spouse, *spouse's name*. If my spouse does not survive me, then I give and bequeath my entire estate to my children in equal shares. If neither my spouse nor any children survive me, then I give and bequeath my entire estate to *name(s) of alternate beneficiary (beneficiaries)*.

ARTICLE V. If I am survived by minor children, their other parent shall serve as Guardian. If the other parent does not survive me, then I appoint *guardian's name* to serve as Guardian.

IN WITNESS WHEREOF, I sign, seal, and publish this Last Will and Testament on this *date* day of *month* 20___.

Your name signed as it appears above

Testator

On the date above, this document was signed, sealed, and published in our presence by the Testator named herein, who declared it to be his/her Last Will and Testament. At the same time, at the request of the Testator, in the Testator's presence, and in the presence of each other, we sign our names as witnesses. We attest that at the time of freely executing this document, we believe the Testator to be of sound mind and under no duress.

Witness signature	*Witness' address*
Witness	Address
Witness signature	*Witness' address*
Witness	Address

Chapter 5

Once made, a will should be placed in a secure place, such as a bank safe deposit box. In many states, the local court house will have an office known as the registrar of wills, where a person can formally file his or her will and have that fact entered in a master index for future reference. The will is kept confidential until the testator's death.

After death, the validity of a will must be proven in a court proceeding known as *probate*. All parties named in the will and all heirs at law of the deceased are notified of this hearing and may then present any objections. The court has the power to interpret the terms of the will and to decide any challenges, always with the main objective of giving full effect to the intentions of the testator.

There are several effective ways to avoid probate (and in some instances, death taxes as well) including the purchase of life insurance policies for named beneficiaries, the creation of living trusts (see page 95), gifts of property during one's lifetime, and holding title to property in forms of joint ownership allowing the right of survivorship.

Comment: One easy way for elderly parents to get around probate is to transfer the title to their residence to their children, reserving a life estate for themselves. This simple expedient substantially reduces the total value of the parents' estate for tax purposes and increases possible Medicaid eligibility. All it takes is the signing of a deed that a lawyer can prepare.

Additional Instructions

A will is essential, but it still leaves many matters for survivors to resolve. Additional written instructions can ease the burden on the executor and family members during a time of grief. Specific burial instructions can be given concerning cemetery plots, or cremation, headstones, or desired ceremony.

(See sample on the next page.)

Your family and heirs will need to know about your personal and business affairs after you are gone. A personal records inventory can help family members locate your important documents and assets in your absence. (See sample on next page.) List all of your bank and other account numbers.

Indicate the location of important documents, such as your birth certificate, tax returns, real estate deeds and product warranties. Also, draw up a list of all your personal advisors (lawyer, accountant, broker, insurance agent, etc.) and their addresses and phone numbers.

Instructions for Funeral and Burial

I, *your name* do hereby direct that upon my death the following wishes to be carried out:

1. It is my wish that my mortal remains be buried in *name and address of cemetery; section number, plot number, and location of deed if already purchased* _____

2. It is my wish that my funeral [or memorial] service be conducted at *name and address of church or funeral home* _____ .

3. It is my wish that the following arrangements be honored: *Instructions for service and name of person who you wish to conduct your service. etc.* _____

Signature: *Your signature* _____   Date: *date*

Instructions for Cremation

I, *your name*, do hereby direct that upon my death my mortal remains be cremated at *name and address of funeral home* and that my ashes be disposed of as follows: *Instructions for disposal*

Signature: *Your signature*   Date: *date*

Detailed funeral instructions should be prepared as a separate document and copies given to your family, executor of your estate named in your will and your attorney.

Chapter 5

Comment: *Assuming your total property estate is relatively simple in its total composition, you can obtain a will form at any stationery or office supply store. Fill it out or copy it yourself according to the accompanying checklist and instructions which will apply your state law. Describe your intentions clearly for your property bequests and devises. Sign it in the presence of a required non-beneficiary witnesses. Then file the original with the registrar of wills, after retaining duplicate copies for your files. By doing this yourself, you will probably save $500 or more in legal fees.*

If the value of your estate is large or there are complicating factors, such as potential tax liability, minor children, or real property located in more than one state, or if you wish to create a testamentary trust, then you will need a lawyer's assistance. The money it will cost for an attorney will be far outweighed by the resulting savings to your estate and your heirs.

A personal records inventory can help family members locate your important documents and assets in you're absence.

Personal Record Inventory

Name: *Your Name*   Date: *date*

Funeral Instructions: *location of documents; who has copies*

Will and Trust(s): *location of documents; who has copies*

Living Will: *location of documents; who has copies*

Power of Attorney: *location of documents; name and address of appointee*

Insurance Policies: *location; names of insurance companies and beneficiaries*

Safe Deposit Box: *location of keys; name and address of bank*

Bank Accounts: *location of checkbooks; account numbers; names addresses of banks*

Stock Certificates: *location; name and address of broker; account number(s)*

IRA, 401k, pension: *location of documents*

Birth Certificate: *location*

Social Security Card: *location; Social Security number*

Passport: *location, passport number*

Premarital Agreement: *location*

Marriage Certificate(s): *location of documents; date and place of marriage (s)*

Divorce Decree(s): *location of documents; date and place of divorce (s)*

Death Certificates: *location of documents; names of deceased*

Tax Returns: *location of documents*

Business Papers: *location and description of documents*

Deeds to Real Estate: *location of documents; list of property*

Mortgage Documents: *location of documents; list of mortgaged property*

Gold/Currency: *location and amount*

Automobile Titles: *location of documents*

Jewelry: *location and description*

Other: *location and description of other documents and/or assets*

2. Trusts

A trust is a legal device allowing title to and possession of property to be held, used, and/or managed by one person (the *trustee*) for the benefit of one or more other persons (the *beneficiaries*).

A trust is one of the most flexible legal mechanisms available in law. A trust can conduct a business; hold title to and invest in real estate, cash, stocks, bonds, negotiable instruments and all sorts of personal property; take care of minors or the elderly; pay medical, educational, or other expenses; provide financial support in retirement, marriage, or divorce; assist in the execution of a premarital agreement; and serve as a major avenue of avoidance for the muddle of probate and the burden of inheritance taxes.

Trust Creation

The person who creates a trust (variously called the *donor*, *grantor*, or *settlor*) conveys legal title of his or her real or personal property or money (the *corpus*) to a third party (the *trustee*). The trustee (who is usually a trusted friend, a professional financial manager, or a bank with a trust department) manages or invests the donor's property or money for the benefit of a named person(s) (the beneficiary). Under the law, legal title and ownership of the trust corpus immediately passes from the grantor to the trust. Control of these assets is vested in the trustee, so long as the trust exists.

The trust beneficiary receives only an equitable title to the income or assets of the trust, as described under the terms of the trust declaration, the basic document authorizing and creating the trust. Powers and duties of a trustee can be broad or narrow according to the declaration, but should carefully reflect the grantor's intentions as to how the trust is to operate.

The grantor may also be the trustee, or one of the trustees, but such arrangements impose a strict duty against self-dealing, lest the validity of the trust itself be called into question.

The Trust Corpus

What assets should go into a trust? Well, if you go to the trouble of creating a trust, an argument can be made that all your assets should be transferred — all real and personal property, including jointly held property. Depending on the consequences, which should be carefully considered, all certificates of stock, securities and other evidences of ownership should be re-issued in the trust name. Bank account titles should be changed from your name to that of the trust. The trust can also be made beneficiary of your life insurance and, in some cases, your pension plans.

For those who value privacy, a trust affords a shield from "prying eyes" and those who might otherwise contest a will during probate. The creation of a trust can be done in such a way that its existence is a matter of public record, but the names of the grantor and the beneficiaries are kept private — and trust assets need not be disclosed.

Types of Trusts

There are numerous types of trusts, each characterized by different variables included in the trust terms, and each with its own advantages, problems and tax results. At various stages of a person's economic life, one or more of these legal devices may be appropriate and, as circumstances change, new ones may well be needed.

Perhaps the greatest use of trusts occurs in estate planning, an effective way of passing title to property, while avoiding both lengthy and complicated probate court procedures, as well as inheritance taxes. Nationally, probate fees (exclusive of death taxes) average from one to 15% of the gross value of the entire estate. Probate in some states (like California) can require up to two years for completion.

A trust, especially if operative for several years, is not likely to be challenged in court. And the existence of a previously created trust is an obvious defense to the charge of mental incompetency, which is often the basis for attacking the validity of a will created late in life.

Testamentary Trust

The most common form of a trust is a testamentary trust, the terms of which the grantor includes in his or her last will to take effect after death. This method allows provisions for loved ones, especially when the grantor has concerns about a minor child beneficiary's ability to manage his or her own affairs. Such concerns have given rise to the testamentary creation of the so-called spendthrift trust, the assets of which are immune from attacks by the beneficiary's personal creditors.

While popular, testamentary trusts have distinct disadvantages often unexplained by legal advisors. For example, estate and income taxes must be paid at the death of the grantor, although proper trust provisions can avoid successive estate tax levies as trust property passes to beneficiaries and their heirs in later years. Also, testamentary trusts do not avoid initial probate and sometimes are subjected to prolonged court supervision, often entailing great legal expense.

Because they are subject to probate, the activity of the testamentary trust and its trustee is a matter of public record for all to see. In order to create a trust other than by a will, the grantor must sign a written declaration or indenture, which gives specific details of the trust operation and its income distribution, both during the grantor's life and afterward. Numerous court and IRS decisions interpreting trust documents have given every clause special meaning. Therefore, the writing of the trust declaration requires expert advice, assistance, and coordination with all other legal arrangements the grantor may have made concerning his or her estate.

Living Trust

A living trust is a trust created while the grantor is alive (known to lawyers as an *inter vivos* trust), also providing for the disposition of the trust assets at the grantor's death. The major benefit is that trust assets avoid probate completely, although they are subject to federal and state estate taxes. In addition to the federal estate tax, 15 states and the District of Columbia have an estate tax, and six states have an inheritance tax. Maryland and New Jersey have both. In contrast to a testamentary trust (which is created after the grantor's death under the terms of a will), a living trust is created by the grantor to take effect and operate immediately, while he or she is still alive.

A *revocable* living trust is an entity to which a grantor voluntarily transfers title to his or her assets, but with a string attached. When a trust is revocable, the grantor retains power during his or her lifetime to vary the trust terms, withdraw assets, or even end the trust entirely by formal invalidation.

There are some real benefits to establishing a revocable living trust. Obviously, the grantor's ability to manage the trust assets during his or her lifetime and the power to end the trust at any time are favorable options. There's also no legal prohibition against the grantor serving as a trustee (or even as a beneficiary) as long as there is one or more additional beneficiaries at the time of the grantor's death. Since the trust can be created in any state jurisdiction (and some states are more hospitable than others), the grantor also has an opportunity to choose the most advantageous law to govern the trust.

A spouse or heirs, as beneficiaries, can benefit greatly from such a trust. In addition to acquiring immediate income from trust assets, beneficiaries gain the following advantages: avoiding judicial probate with the attendant expense and time delays (trust property is not included in the grantor's personal estate); allowing the uninterrupted operation of a family business placed in trust; avoiding public scrutiny of personal financial matters; causing no temporary stop in income for beneficiaries during probate after death.

The biggest disadvantage of a revocable trust is that it provides very little asset protection. Federal and state trust law generally restricts the nature and extent of benefits and control that a grantor can retain after creating his or her trust. When a grantor retains any degree of control over assets allegedly transferred to a trust, then those assets may still remain within ultimate reach of the grantor's creditors.

In 10 states (Alabama, Indiana, Kansas, Michigan, Minnesota, North Dakota, Ohio, Oklahoma, South Dakota, and Wisconsin) there are laws which declare that a grantor who retains an absolute power of revocation is deemed to be the owner of the trust property for the purpose of creditors and purchasers. Case law in many other states has opened revocable trust arrangements to similar creditor attachment.

As a general rule, this incestuous game of same grantor/trustee/beneficiary can be risky. Such a cozy arrangement is sure to be challenged by creditors, many of which are often successful.

Irrevocable Trusts

A living trust may also be expressly created as "irrevocable," denying a grantor ultimate control (after the trust is created) over the assets transferred to the trust. There are many legitimate reasons for the creation of such a trust, including logical estate planning, making reasonable provisions for spouse and children, and the like.

As a protection against asset attachment, this is virtually perfect, because the donor no longer has title to the property or any ability to re-acquire it. The only possibility of a successful attack by creditors might occur if the transfer can be proven to be fraudulent in some way.

Irrevocability is the trust's unique feature and a court which finds irrevocability will usually confirm the trust assets are shielded from the grantor's creditors. But irrevocability is also a major disadvantage — if circumstances change, the trust cannot be changed to meet them.

> **Comment:** *If you want to create a trust, you need an excellent trust lawyer and/or tax lawyer who can draft a trust declaration suitable to your objectives. This is definitely not a do-it-yourself project.*

3. Joint Ownership

Joint ownership is probably the most prevalent form of family property ownership in the United States, with an estimated three-fourths of all real estate owned by married couples held in some form of joint tenancy. Stocks, bonds, bank accounts, autos, boats and numerous other items of personal property are also jointly owned — not just by husbands and wives, but by virtually unlimited combinations of family and non-family multi-party ownership. This is no doubt an accurate reflection of the enormous diversity of personal and business relationships existing in our modern society.

Joint ownership can be used to avoid probate entirely for part of a person's property or, more appropriately, it can supplement a will or trust arrangement.

THE CASE OF THE IRREVOCABLE INSURANCE

When their youngest son, Carlos, turned 15, Juan and Maria decided it was time to do some estate planning. Their financial advisor suggested shifting money to Carlos and his older sister, Christina, age 21, in the form of insurance trusts. This would reduce the size of Juan and Maria's estate and exposure to probate, estate taxes and attack by creditors. The trusts could also serve as a source of college funds if Juan and Maria are unable to afford tuition down the road.

Juan and Maria created an irrevocable trust for each child, each containing a life insurance policy. The insurance company was willing to pay the $1,500 in legal fees since the policies were purchased from them. Maria's younger sister, Anna, a lawyer, agreed to serve as trustee for her nephew and niece.

Each life insurance policy has an initial death benefit of $1.4 million. Juan and Maria can contribute up to $20,000 annually in policy premiums free of any gift tax. They put $20,000 a year in for five years. Because they chose "variable" insurance, Juan and Maria are able to direct how the money is invested — in this case, they invested it in several mutual funds. About 20 to 30% of the premium goes for insurance fees in the first year, and a "surrender fee" must be paid if the policy is cashed in before its 10th anniversary.

The trust stipulates that when each child reaches the age of 35, he or she becomes the owner of the life insurance policy outright. The insurance company projects an annual return of more than 10%, even after all fees are paid. Based on that assumption, Christina's policy will be worth $379,880 when she turns age 35. Then she has the option of terminating the policy — but will have to pay a capital gains tax on her investment profit of $279,880 — or she can use the policy as an investment vehicle by keeping it in force, designating the beneficiary as she sees fit, and borrowing against the policy's value if she needs cash. In addition, Carlos' policy will be worth $700,003 by the age of 35 and would have to pay capital gains tax on $600,003 if he cancelled the policy.

Joint Tenancy

In a *joint tenancy* arrangement, two or more people own property jointly and equally unless otherwise apportioned by agreement. The distinguishing feature is the *right of survivorship*, which means that at the death of one joint tenant, the other joint tenant or tenants automatically receive ownership of the share of the deceased without having to go through probate.

There are some potential problems created by a joint tenancy. For example, a joint tenant can dispose of his or her joint interest without the consent of the other owner. Also, joint tenancy offers no protection from creditors and, during a joint tenant's life, his or her interest is subject to attachment for debts. However, since joint tenancy contains the right of survivorship, the creditors of the deceased joint owner cannot reach the property after death unless the joint ownership was expressly created to defraud creditors of the deceased, or for payment of federal or state taxes owed by the deceased.

In the case of joint bank accounts, depending on state law, joint ownership may or may not protect a joint tenant from attachment for debts of the other joint owner. In many states, the creditor has a right to the debtor's one-half interest, or if one party contributed all or most of the money in the account, the creditor can obtain all the funds. Under federal bankruptcy law, the interest of a joint tenant is highly vulnerable once he or she files for bankruptcy, and creditors obtain increased collection rights against such property.

Chapter 5

THE CASE OF THE GEORGETOWN JOINT TENANTS

Forty years ago, two industrious do-it-yourselfers named Rod and Bob wanted to open an antiques business in Washington, D.C. They bought a run-down 25-room mansion in the decaying city section known as Georgetown. The deed granting ownership of the house made them joint tenants with the right of survivorship. Rod and Bob remained partners while Georgetown transformed itself into the ritziest section of the nation's capital city.

After a long life and successful career in the antiques business, Bob died and carelessly failed to make a will. Since Rod and Bob had established joint tenancy, however, Rod has no problem settling Bob's estate and pays no estate taxes. Rod automatically becomes sole owner of the show-case house and business, now worth millions of dollars.

Comment: Although holding title to property in joint tenancy does not offer much protection against creditors, it does avoid probate. Twenty-four states legally recognize tenancy by the entireties, which is essentially a form of joint tenancy ownership of property available only to a husband and wife. As in the case of a joint tenancy, the right of survivorship goes to the surviving spouse, automatically and without the need for probate — although estate taxes may be owed.

Tenancy by the Entireties

This form of joint ownership owes its existence to the common law theory that a man and woman united in matrimony become — in the eyes of the law — one person (i.e., a "unity"). According to this view, two people do not own the property, but the single legal "person" created by the unity of marriage owns it. Because of this unity, neither party can convey away the property without the consent of the other, or until one party dies or the marriage is dissolved. Unless the property was jointly pledged by both parties to obtain a loan or other credit, or unless some other debt was jointly incurred by both parties, the deceased party's creditors have no rights to the property upon the death of the debtor. However, if any debt is a joint debt of both husband and wife, the property is open to creditor attachment.

Tax Consequences

Depending on the total value of the estate of a husband and wife, holding property in joint tenancy or a tenancy in the entireties can have costly estate tax consequences. When jointly held property passes at death by law to a surviving spouse, it becomes part of that spouse's taxable estate. This means the $5.43 million (2015) *marital tax exemption* allowed on the estate of the dead spouse goes unused. Equally bad is the fact that the tax liability of the remaining spouse's estate eventually increases.

If the husband and wife are of modest means and do not expect to have a joint estate valued in excess of $5.43 million, no tax savings are at risk. But since the median average price of a home is $212,000 at this writing (2015), the great majority of couples could be hit with increased taxes as a result of joint ownership when one spouse dies.

Under current tax law, a surviving spouse has nine months to file a "qualified disclaimer" when left everything by a deceased spouse. This is usually done as an estate planning move in order to take advantage of the $3.5 million marital exemption.

Under joint ownership, the disclaimer is not available. Check with your tax advisor. Rather than joint ownership, the best course of action may be for a husband and wife to divide family assets into two chunks as nearly equal as possible.

Community Property

In nine states (Arizona, California, Idaho, Louisiana, New Mexico, Nevada, Texas, Washington, and Wisconsin) a form of joint ownership by husband and wife (known as *community property*) is recognized by law. In this arrangement, each spouse owns one half of all jointly owned property, and their rights are approximately the same as joint tenants, with the ability to sell or encumber their interest during life. However, there is no survivorship at death, and if a spouse dies intestate, the community property interest is passed to heirs either under state law (which varies greatly), or it can be willed.

The laws of community property states vary greatly as to creditors' rights against spouses individually and jointly, or against "community property" itself, which has a complex definition. As a general rule, planned asset protection must be dealt with separately and apart from marriage in such states.

4. Living Wills, Powers of Attorney, and Guardianships

Unfortunately, situations can occur that result in the inability of a person to make competent decisions. This condition is usually associated with serious illness or injury, often rendering a person unable even to communicate his or her wishes.

In recent years, several publicized legal cases have been decided by courts regarding the "right to die," and laws on the subject have been enacted in almost every state. In 1993, a federal law required all hospitals receiving any form of U.S. government payment (including Medicare and Medicaid) to provide prospective patients with full information about their rights to control their own medical treatment — and to choose to refuse such treatment should they reach a terminal condition.

There are now several recognized documentary forms available to a person who wishes to control his or her medical treatment when he or she may become mentally or physically incapacitated.

Living Wills & Health Care Proxies

A living will is a document written and signed by a person expressing exactly what medical treatment he or she wishes if he or she becomes unable to make competent decisions or is in a terminal or persistent vegetative state. Usually, the document will state that the person's preference whether or not to receive any life-prolonging treatment if the situation becomes medically hopeless. (See sample on page 103.)

A living will is nothing more than a person's expression of a preference, and usually family members or a hospital doctor decide the point at which the medical condition the patient foresaw is reached.

Understandably, health care providers are reluctant to move too quickly in carrying out a wish to be allowed to die.

Far more useful is a document lawyers call a durable power of attorney for health care (also known as a health care proxy or an advance directive), in which a person gives the full legal power to another person to make health care decisions, if he or she is unable to do so. The "durable" aspect of the document is that the power given to its holder remains operative even if he or she becomes totally incapacitated.

This document can and should contain specific instructions as to the subject's wishes, even down to naming specific diseases and conditions and directing what should be done in each case. The person holding the power of attorney has the sole right to make the health care decisions required, and medical personnel are obliged to follow that person's instructions. Treatment is not left to chance, once a terminal or vegetative state diagnosis is rendered.

> **Comment:** *Forms for advance directives complying with state law are usually available from local hospitals or other health care facilities, or from your doctor. The forms are relatively simple, and you can write one to your own specifications. Be sure to sign it with witnesses (if state law requires) and keep it in a place where it can easily be obtained if a medical emergency occurs. Copies of such directives should always be provided to a hospital if you are checking in for any medical purpose, however minor.*

Guardianship

Assuming a person has not had the foresight to execute an advance directive regarding health care, or a general durable power of attorney, the law does allow a court to appoint a guardian for a person no longer able to make his or her own decisions due to mental or physical incapacity.

The court, upon a petition reciting the facts of the person's disability, can appoint someone (usually next of kin or the per-

Living Will Declaration

This declaration is made this *date* day of *month*, 20___

I, *full legal name*, being an adult of sound mind, do willfully and voluntarily let this statement stand as an expression of my wishes and directions, if the time comes when I can no longer take part in decisions regarding my own future.

If at any time I should have a terminal condition as diagnosed by at least two (2) physicians who have personally examined me, one of whom shall be my attending physician, where the application of life-prolonging procedures would serve only to artificially prolong my death, I direct that such procedures be withheld or withdrawn, and that I be permitted to die naturally with only the administration of medication or the performance of medical procedures deemed necessary to provide me with comfort care or to alleviate pain.

I [do] [do not] desire that nutrition and hydration be withheld or withdrawn when the application of such procedures would serve only to artificially prolong my death.

In the absence of my ability to give directions regarding the use of such life-prolonging procedures, it is my intention that this declaration shall be honored by my family and physicians as the final expression of my legal right to refuse medical or surgical treatment, and I accept the consequences of such refusal.

This declaration shall remain in effect unless and until it is revoked by me. I understand that I may revoke this declaration at any time. This declaration shall be governed by the laws of the state of *your state*

I understand the full importance of this declaration, and I am emotionally and mentally competent to make this declaration.

your name signed as it appears above   *Your City*
Declarant   City of Residence

                                                 Your County
                                                 County of Residence

                                                 Your State
                                                 State of Residence

The Declarant is known to me, and I believe him/her to be of sound mind.

_____   *First Witness' signature*
Date   Witness

_____   *Second Witness' signature*
Date   Witness

A living will expresses exactly what medical treatment a person wishes if he or she becomes incompetent to make decisions or is in a persistent vegetative state.

Chapter 5

son's attorney) to conduct the disabled person's business and other affairs during the disability. "Disability" in this sense means any legal incapacity and, thus, a court can appoint a guardian for a minor child (known as a "ward") who inherits an estate.

Power of Attorney

Quite apart from health care or other emergencies, a person has the power to transfer to another person either full or qualified powers to act on his or her behalf, just as if the person were acting for himself or herself. A limited or special power of attorney allows a person to act as agent for another person in specific described circumstances, as in a real estate settlement, or in handling a particular bank account. Or, a person can give a general power of attorney, allowing another to do everything the person could do, as when the person may be out of the country for an extended period of time. If a power of attorney contains a durable power, it will state that the power granted will continue even if the person giving it becomes incapacitated or disabled, terminating only with death. (See sample on next page.) Any of these powers of attorney must be in written form and, in many states, they must be witnessed or notarized.

Comment: The legal forms necessary to create a power of attorney are relatively simple to fill out or copy, requiring only the signatures of the person giving the power, witnesses, and, in some states, a notary. If the power is limited, be sure to state the exact limitations imposed. This is a case where you can usually do it yourself without a lawyer.

General Durable Power of Attorney

BE IT KNOWN, that I, *name of person granting authority*, the undersigned Principal, hereby grant this General Durable Power of Attorney to *name of person receiving authority*, as my attorney-in-fact.

My attorney-In-fact shall have full power and authority to do any and all acts on my behalf that I could do personally including but not limited to:

The right to sell, deed, buy, trade, lease mortgage, assign, rent, or dispose of any of my present or future real or personal property;

The right to execute, accept, undertake, and perform any and all contracts in my name;

The right to deposit, endorse, or withdraw funds to or from any of my bank accounts or safe-deposit boxes; the right to borrow, collect, lend, invest, or reinvest funds on any terms;

The right to initiate, defend, commence, or settle legal actions on my behalf;

The right to vote (in person or by proxy) any shares or beneficial interest in any entity; and the right to retain any accountant, attorney, or other advisor deemed necessary to protect my interests relative to any foregoing unlimited power.

My attorney-in-fact hereby accepts this appointment subject to its terms and agrees to act and perform in a fiduciary capacity consistent with my best Interests as my attorney-in-fact in his/her best discretion deems advisable, and I affirm and ratify all acts so undertaken.

This Power of Attorney may be revoked by me at any time, and shall automatically be revoked upon my death, provided any person relying on this Power of Attorney shall have full rights to accept the authority of my attorney-in-fact until in receipt of actual notice of revocation. It is my intention that this instrument be construed as a Durable Power of Attorney, and that it shall not be affected by my subsequent disability or incapacity. A photocopy of this Power of Attorney shall be deemed an original for all purposes permitted by law.

Signed this *date* day of *month*, 20___

Principal's signature

Principal

I accept appointment as attorney-in-fact as granted by this Power of Attorney.

Attorney-In-Fact's signature

Attorney-In-Fact

[NOTARY'S STATEMENT AND SEAL]

A general durable power of attorney is granted by someone who wishes to transfer the management of his or her property and financial affairs to another person whom they trust.

Chapter 5

CHAPTER 6:
THE LAW OF TORTS

It is a reasonable assumption that as long as there has been human interaction on Earth, people have injured each other and damaged each other's property, either accidentally or on purpose.

The law governing such unfortunate events is known as the *law of torts*. "Torts" is an ancient English word adopted from the French word meaning "wrong" and, in turn, derived from the Latin word *tortum* meaning, literally, "twisted."

The basic concept of tort law holds one person responsible for injuring another or for damaging another's property. The person who commits the wrong must pay money to the injured person, as recompense for the damage caused. Generally, wrongful (or "tortious") conduct fits into three categories: 1) *negligence*, 2) *intentional misconduct* and 3) conduct for which the law imposes *strict liability*.

A tort involves an individual who has been wronged and who seeks money damages in a civil lawsuit that he or she chooses to file. In a criminal situation, however, society as a whole (the state) brings a person to justice for committing an intentional act forbidden by law and imposes a punishment of a fine or imprisonment, or both. In some cases, the same act may have dual consequences, both civil tort and criminal liability. For example, rape is a crime for which the tort equivalents are assault and battery, false imprisonment and infliction of emotional distress.

> **Comment:** *Tort law is an area of complex, fact-intensive legal intricacies developed over centuries and not easily mastered, even by attorneys. In tort cases, lawyers usually offer their services on a contingent fee basis, meaning they do not charge a client unless and until the matter is successfully settled, either by compromise or by a court verdict. Such cases usually require two or more years to come to trial and reach a verdict and appeals can take even longer.*

If a lawyer loses a case, the client pays only the costs of the suit (such as filing fees), but no lawyer's fees. If the lawyer wins, the lawyer collects one-quarter to one-third of the total amount of damages awarded (plus costs), depending on whether the case was settled out of court or had to go to trial.

Most attorneys will provide a potential client a free initial consultation in a tort case, allowing the client a reasonable assessment of the merits of the case. At the inception of a tort case, with so much at stake, it is best to obtain the professional opinion of an experienced tort lawyer.

Calculating Compensation

Money compensation paid in most tort cases is called *damages* and is measured in monetary awards. Damages can be *compensatory* (paying for the actual cost of the harm) or *punitive* (additional amounts awarded as punishment in more extreme cases). In a personal injury case damages consist of: 1) *special damages* (provable costs associated with the tort, such as lost wages, medical expenses and hospital bills); 2) *compensation for pain and suffering;* and, 3) compensation for amounts which compensate for permanent disability or injury.

In cases in which a defendant has caused a wrongful death, the spouse and children of the deceased are entitled to special damages (described above), plus an amount reflecting the prospective loss resulting from the death. This includes a spouse's loss of consortium (love, companionship, and services) and future economic loss based on what the deceased would have earned in a normal lifetime.

The actual amount of damages awarded in a case is decided by a jury, based on the facts presented at trial. If a jury verdict is excessive or otherwise inconsistent with the facts and law, the judge can set the award aside, modify it, or order a new trial.

1. Negligence

Most tort cases involve negligence, defined as the failure of a person to exercise the *due care* that an *ordinary reasonable and prudent person* owes others under similar circumstances. Such unreasonable acts become the *proximate cause* of injury to another person or to property.

Negligence can be the basis for a civil suit if the injured person can prove all of the following: 1) the accused person had a duty of care toward the injured person, 2) he or she breached that duty by his or her acts, 3) the breach was the proximate cause of the injury, and 4) the injury resulted in a measurable loss to the injured person.

Proximate cause is defined as any injury-producing act or omission having the likely (therefore, *foreseeable*) result of causing such injury. The negligent act need not be the direct or immediate cause of the injury in order to be "proximate" and impose liability so long as the negligent act is the *efficient cause* ("efficient" in the sense of "cause and effect"), and there is no *intervening cause* between that act and the ultimate injury. Thus, one can be liable for negligence because of an original act setting in motion a chain of events which, when combined, caused injury.

Tort law defines the *reasonable person* as an average adult of unspecified age without physical or mental disabilities, who is cautious without being excessively careful. When judging what is reasonable, each individual's limitations must be taken into account. Children, the elderly and people with disabilities are measured by a different standard of care, since they may have more of a propensity to act negligently.

The *duty of care* (how much care is owed to the injured party) is decided by a jury at trial after all relevant evidence is presented. This means that, in a negligence case, there usually is a valid dispute over what is "reasonable" conduct under a given set of conditions.

When no explanation of an alleged negligent act can be found, tort law applies a doctrine known as *res ipsa loquitur*, which is Latin for "the thing speaks for itself." This notion applies only when the accused party had exclusive control over the situation, the injured party did not contribute to his or her own injury, and the accident would not have happened unless someone was negligent. Under this doctrine, for example, when a commercial airplane crashes, killing all aboard, the airline is presumed negligent in the absence of any other explanation. (However, an international treaty "*The Unification of Certain*

Rules for International Carriage by Air," known as The Montreal Convention, governs and may limit airline liability for injuries or death to passengers during most international flights.)

The Meaning of Proximate Cause

Determination of proximate cause includes deciding the duty, if any, a defendant owes to an injured person, the reasonable foresee-ability of the injurious event, whether other's actions contributed or superseded the original act as the cause, and, therefore, whether the injury was a direct or indirect consequence of the defendant's act.

One of the classic cases concerning proximate cause taught in law schools and quoted by courts is *Palzgraf* v. *Long Island Railroad Co.*, 248 N. W. 162, 162 N.E. 99 (1928), a New York decision written by the great jurist, later U. S. Supreme Court justice, Benjamin Cardozo.

In this case, a man named Palzgraf was standing on a platform of the Long Island Railroad, while another passenger a great distance away was rushing to board a departing train. Two of the railroad's employees tried to help the hurrying person to get aboard, but in so doing dislodged a package from the person's hands. The package, which contained fireworks, caused an enormous explosion on impact. In the ensuing panic, a heavy metal scale on the platform was knocked over, injuring the hapless Palzgraf, who sued the railroad for negligence on the theory that the employees' conduct caused the injury.

The court, in a controversial 4-3 decision, emphasized the concept of a defendant's duty of care, concluding the railroad could not possibly have foreseen this complex chain of events and, therefore, owed no duty of care to Palzgraf. Since there was no duty established, there could be no breach of duty. Therefore there was no legal negligence and no proximate cause.

So, in effect, proximate cause means what a court applying the law and a jury assessing the facts say it means. This has led to the suggestion that the phrase be replaced with illegal cause, so as to avoid the confusion the use of the word proximate (meaning near in time and space) has produced in generations of judges, tort lawyers and clients.

Defenses to Negligence

Even when a person is negligent, depending on the facts, the law of torts allows several defenses to remove any liability for the original negligence.

Many years ago, the law of almost every state held that if the party complaining of a negligent injury was himself guilty of any degree of negligence contributing to his injury, he could recover nothing from the other party. This strict doctrine of *contributory negligence* still applies in Maryland, the District of Columbia, Alabama, North Carolina and Virginia.

Forty-five other states (and Puerto Rico and the U.S. Virgin Islands) apply the rule of *comparative negligence*, allowing either party to recover damages, but only to the estimated degree each party is found to have been negligent. Under this rule, so long as the injured party's negligence is less than that of the wrong-doer, he or she can recover some damages.

In many states, if the injured party's own negligence is equal to or greater than that of the defendant, no recovery is allowed. In other states, any negligence by the defendant, even the slightest degree, can be the basis of a limited award of damages.

In some states, the *doctrine of last clear chance* applies. It holds that even though the person injured may have exposed himself or herself to the harm (thus being guilty of contributory negligence), the injured party can recover damages against a defendant who was aware of the peril to the other party, and yet failed to take action that could have prevented the harm. This is often the case in auto accident litigation.

Another defense to alleged negligence is *assumption of risk*. Thus, when a voluntary spectator at a baseball game is hit by a fly ball, he has no right to sue since he knew, or should have known, that such accidents do happen at baseball games. Any person who voluntarily places himself in harm's way assumes the risk.

2. Intentional Torts

In these torts, the critical element is the state of mind of the person who causes the injury. If a person deliberately causes harm, the tort is intentional. The major difference between an intentional tort and negligence is that the injured party has, in addition to all other damages, a right to punitive damages, designed to punish and deter the wrongdoer.

Here is a list of intentional torts:

- **Assault:** a deliberate act that causes a person at whom it is directed to fear, or have apprehension of, the immediate danger of being harmed. No actual physical contact is required — only the perceived threat.

- **Battery:** a deliberate striking or touching of another person without his or her permission, even if no physical harm results. This does not include a parent or, in many states, a teacher using non-injurious limited force against a child for disciplinary purposes.

- **False imprisonment:** the illegal confinement of a person against his or her will with no way to escape, a situation that often arises in mistaken or false arrests. This need not involve physical barriers — force or the threat of force is enough in many cases.

- **Malicious prosecution:** the filing of a civil suit or the making of a criminal complaint against a person, when there are no valid grounds to do so. A related tort is "abuse of process," which is the abuse of the judicial process, such as filing a suit without merit as a means of harassment.

- **Fraud:** the intentional making of a false statement of fact (not opinion) known to the maker to be untrue, with knowledge that the hearer will rely on the misrepresentation.

- **Invasion of privacy:** includes unreasonable intrusion into a person's private life, making public the facts about a person's private life, falsely portraying a person to the public and using a person's name or picture for commercial purposes without his or her consent.

- **Defamation:** a false statement about a person which damages his or her reputation. When this is done in spoken words, it is the tort of slander. When the defamation is in writing, it is libel. In either case, some third person must read or hear the defamatory statement, before a tort occurs.

- **Emotional distress:** causing a person to suffer mental or emotional distress, usually to such a degree that physical harm results.

- **Trespass to chattels:** the lawyer's way of saying intentional damage to, or interference with, a person's personal property (or "chattels"). A related tort is "conversion," the destruction or stealing of another's personal property.

- **Trespass to real property:** a person's going onto, or remaining on, the real property of another person, without the express or implied consent of the owner or the owner's agent, even if no damage results. An owner may use "reasonable force" to eject a trespasser, but has a duty to avoid inflicting intentional harm and to warn of any existing dangerous conditions known to the owner. A similar duty of warning about known dangers is owed by an owner to invited guests. If a person can be classified as a "business visitor," such as a delivery person or a customer, the owner has a continuing duty to keep the premises safe and/or warn of any known dangers.

3. Strict Liability

The central element in this kind of tort is not reckless conduct or intention, but the inherently hazardous nature of the act itself.

Under tort law, certain conduct is considered to be so extremely dangerous that when injury results from such activities, damages can be recovered without having to prove anyone did anything wrong. Strict liability would apply to personal injury or property damage caused by such events as a fireworks display gone awry, a toxic chemical spill, shock waves or debris from building demolition or blasting with explosives or the explosion of a nuclear power plant.

Medical Malpractice

One of the major points in the national debate over the alleged need for health care "reform" has been the issue of medical malpractice lawsuits and their cost to the economy. Doctors and other medical personnel contend contrived lawsuits against them for alleged professional mistakes are driving them out of business — and adding billions to health care costs. Trial lawyers and plaintiffs' advocates argue for the right to be compensated for medical mistakes. The 2010 Affordable Care Act (ACA), "Obamacare" did not address this controversial political issue.

Medical malpractice definitely is a problem. The *Harvard Medical Practice Study*, a review comparing medical injuries and malpractice claims filed in the State of New York, attributes as many as 300,000 "bad outcomes" annually to "physician error."

This number includes over 80,000 deaths, which is more than the number of deaths in the U.S. resulting from auto accidents and AIDS combined.

The same much-quoted study found that while more than 80% of the medical malpractice claims filed showed no harm done (much less negligence), fewer than 3% of those who actually are injured by health-care professionals ever file suit. The 40 million Americans at or near poverty level were identified as the single group most likely to suffer from medical malpractice.

Medical malpractice falls within the area of tort law covering negligence. In a medical situation, the health care provider has a *duty of care* toward the patient. If that duty of care is breached and is the proximate cause of injury, the patient can recover for the injury — or his next of kin can recover for wrongful death.

Since medicine is not an exact science, not every unfortunate result of medical treatment constitutes malpractice. But a health care provider must possess and use a degree of learning, skill and care in diagnosing and treating a patient that any reasonable, competent, similar health care provider would apply under like circumstances.

Whenever a doctor's treatment falls below that common standard, he or she has committed medical malpractice. In some cases, the malpractice is clear. For example, a surgeon leaves a sponge in a patient's abdominal wall after an operation, resulting in prolonged infection; or a surgeon amputates the wrong finger. In other cases, the issue is not so clear. For instance, a patient suffers serious post-operative problems resulting in death, and his family claims the doctor never told him this could occur.

The same standard of due care extends to diagnosis, as well as treatment. This means a doctor must obtain the patient's full medical history and a complete description of all current symptoms. All appropriate tests should be conducted to support or confirm a diagnosis.

If a doctor provides an incorrect diagnosis, he or she can be held responsible for any resulting injury to the patient, as well as for any pain and suffering it may have caused. Liability would occur when a simple problem is diagnosed as more serious than it is, requiring erroneous extensive and painful treatment — or when a serious condition is misdiagnosed, resulting in a worsening of the condition.

The Case of the Injured Gymnast

For years, a prize-winning gymnast named Jennifer had great hopes for the Olympics. One day, in a nasty fall from the balance beam, she tore worn cartilage in her knee, made fragile by her many years of athletic activity.

Dr. Thompson, an orthopedic surgeon, treated the young woman first with physical therapy and anti-inflammatory drugs. When that treatment proved ineffective and the pain continued, Dr. Thompson performed arthroscopic surgery, entering the knee through a small incision and attempting to repair the damaged cartilage. Unfortunately, the pain worsened, and Jennifer's Olympic dreams were quickly fading.

By chance, a friend of Jennifer's mentioned that she had heard of a doctor named Dr. Jackson who recommends a new Swiss-researched knee procedure that transplants healthy cartilage from a patient's other bones to damaged joints, where it can regenerate and restore a damaged knee to excellent health. Jennifer sees Dr. Jackson, who ended up performing the procedure successfully.

Can Jennifer sue Dr. Thompson for medical malpractice for failing to recommend the innovative Swiss surgical procedure? The answer is yes. And Jennifer may very well win her case.

If a doctor believes a patient's medical condition is beyond his or her expertise and requires diagnosis by a specialist, the doctor has a duty to refer the patient immediately to a second doctor. Failure to do so would result in the initial doctor's being held liable for any consequences that may occur.

The law requires a health care provider to have and maintain a continuing degree of learning, skill and care in diagnosis and treatment that any reasonable and competent similar health care provider would apply under similar circumstances. Part of the required degree of skill means keeping up with all new developments in a doctor's medical specialty so that patients can benefit from the latest treatments.

Similarly, if a doctor recommends a certain treatment or surgery, you have an absolute right to a second opinion before you consent. The doctor must, as a matter of law, inform you of all the ramifications of your condition, including any risks associated with treatment, or alternative treatments, so that you can give *informed consent.*

Patient's Rights

Although few situations in life require a person to reveal intimate details to another person, medical treatment routinely imposes this sometimes unpleasant task. As a result, the law requires a doctor to keep absolutely confidential the facts he or she learns about a patient — unless the patient consents to having them revealed. This is called the doctor-patient privilege.

There are exceptions to this rule. In some states, health care providers must report suspected child abuse to government agencies or to the police. People with certain infectious diseases, such as hepatitis or tuberculosis, must by law be reported to state health authorities. Almost all doctors require that their patients sign consent forms allowing the doctor to give the details of each person's medical condition to insurance companies for the purposes of obtaining "third party" payment.

Most states now require health care providers to provide copies of their medical records to patients who request them, for a reasonable copying charge.

A major privacy issue has arisen in recent years because of proposed national patient databases that would contain everyone's medical records and be available at any medical facility.

Proponents argue that this would be more efficient. Opponents fear the adverse use of personal medical information by employers or insurance companies. Data base system proposals such as this are a part of various "health care reform" bills pending in the U.S. Congress at this writing.

Under U.S. Department of Health and Human Services (HHS) rules implementing the 2010 Affordable Care Act (ACA) state, federal and local agencies as well as health insurers are required to swap the protected personal health information of anybody seeking Obamacare insurance on an exchange and that includes an individual's medical history, test and laboratory results, insurance information and other data. It seems that privacy is lost.

Must a doctor accept you as a patient? Usually not, except in an emergency situation requiring immediate medical treatment due to a life-threatening condition. This emergency treatment requirement extends to hospitals, without regard to a showing of a patient's prior proof of ability to pay.

Do patients have the right to choose to die? We all will eventually exercise this right one way or another, but in recent years the debate has been whether or not a doctor or anyone has the right to assist a terminally ill patient in taking his or her own life.

Assisted suicide remains a crime in most states. In a 1994 referendum, Oregon voters narrowly approved the first law allowing doctor-certified terminally ill patients to request and self-administer lethal doses of medication. Four other states, Montana, New Mexico, Vermont and Washington, now allow for medically assisted death.

In 2006, the United States Supreme Court sided with Oregon in upholding the nation's first physician-assisted suicide law. Oregon voters had twice upheld the law that permits the terminally ill to take an overdose of drugs if two doctors agree with the diagnosis and conclude the patient is of sound mind. The patient must clearly show this to be his or her informed wish. Since the law was passed in 1997, a total of 1,327 people have availed themselves of medically assisted suicide.

Check Chapter 5 on *living wills* and *health care powers of attorney* for ways to ensure that your wishes are carried out on exactly what medical treatment you would like in the unfortunate event that you become unable to make competent decisions or fall into a terminal or persistent vegetative state.

CHAPTER 7:
PROPERTY RIGHTS — REAL, PERSONAL AND MIXED

1. Real Estate

The law of real estate (or real property) covers almost as much territory as there are square miles of land. Real estate is land and anything growing or erected on the land that is permanently attached and cannot be moved. In some states, real estate even includes underwater areas of river and lake beds and oceanfront to the mean low water mark, all considered to be part of adjacent dry land.

Because land is so valuable, especially in urban areas, the legal methods by which ownership is signified and transferred are precise, subject to numerous laws that must be followed in order for a buyer to obtain a valid title.

For most people, the most significant event involving real estate law is the purchase or sale of a home. In this highly mobile society, real estate sale and purchase procedures vary greatly in different geographic areas, although the fundamentals are the same.

Buying or Selling a House

For example, in some areas, the entire transaction is handled by the seller's real estate agent and a title and escrow company. In other areas, both parties are represented by attorneys, the buyer's lawyer does a title search before settlement, and the real estate agent has only a minor role.

In most cases, an owner lists his or her home with a *real estate broker*, who advertises it for sale, shows it to prospective buyers, and helps negotiate the sale. In some areas, a first formal step occurs when the seller and buyer sign a binder, a short statement of agreement of sale at a stated price under terms to be spelled out in a *contract of sale* to be signed within a few days. The binder, usually accompanied by a small deposit from the buyer, has the effect of taking the house off the market immediately and holding it for the buyer.

All sellers and their agents would prefer to have a binder, but the best course of action for a purchaser is to ask for a completed contract of sale as the first document both parties sign. This document is the blueprint for the purchase, spelling out in great detail the obligations of both parties, along with any contingencies that may cause the sale to be cancelled including the buyers not obtaining proper financing, acceptable termite and building inspections or a clear, marketable title. The contract will usually be accompanied by a substantial deposit from the seller (say $1,000 or more, depending on the total purchase price), which should always be refundable.

The contract of sale should include: full names and addresses of the seller and the buyer; the purchase price and deposit; a list of all contingencies, the most important of which is the terms of financing the buyer wishes to obtain; a list of all personal property that stays with the house (drapes, carpets, appliances, etc.); requirements for repairs and inspections; a statement of the seller's duty to convey a "good and merchantable title"; broker's fees, tax, utility, and other adjustments; a date by which the seller must vacate the premises; and the settlement date.

Once the contract of sale is signed, an *escrow account* is established, either by one of the party's lawyers or by a title company that will examine the title and issue a title insurance policy, once clear title is established. A *good and marketable title* is what every seller must be able to give, and what every buyer must have — meaning the title search of official public land and tax records finds no legal defects or other encumbrances on the land or buildings.

What sort of legal defects? Title problems can include, among other things: covenants or restrictions in prior deeds limiting the use of the land; improper or inaccurate legal description of the geographic land area itself; encroachments by adjoining landowners; easements giving others rights of way or access to the land; judgments, or federal or state tax liens owed by the seller; liens filed by trades people who have done work on the property and have not been paid; unpaid real estate taxes; or even a petition in bankruptcy by the seller. If the land has been mortgaged, the balance owed on the existing mortgage must be paid off at the settlement before the purchaser can obtain a clear title.

If there are no defects in the title, the seller, buyer, a representative of the financing institution (assuming the buyer does not pay the entire price in cash) and the real estate agent meet for the final *settlement* or *closing*, as it is called. Money and a deed are exchanged, and a new mortgage is signed by the buyer after evidence both parties have met their obligations under the contract of sale. All these formalities can also be handled by attorneys representing the seller and buyer.

Buying or Selling a House without a Broker or Agent

Step 1: Buyer finds a desirable property and makes an offer.

Step 2: Seller accepts the offer.

Step 3: A written contract of sale is signed by both parties, spelling out details and contingencies (including financing terms, seller's guarantees of good and marketable title, etc.).

Step 4: Buyer seeks and obtains desired financing from lender.

Step 5: Buyer's attorney or title company examines title and issues title insurance.

Step 6: Buyer's attorney prepares deed and settlement papers and checks fulfillment of all contingencies in contract of sale.

Step 7: At the closing the buyer, seller, and lender (or their representatives) exchange money, deed, and mortgage papers.

Step 8: Signed deed and mortgage are filed by attorney in official land records.

Step 9: Seller vacates, and buyer takes possession of property.

A tax tip for home sellers: Under the 1997 Tax Act, depending on certain tests of ownership and the period owned, up to $250,000 of the sale price can be tax exempt, or $500,000 for a couple, allowing the sellers to avoid any capital gains tax on the sale.

Building a New Home

The same basic procedure applies when a buyer orders a new home built by a contractor. In addition to the usual features in a contract of sale for an existing house, there are written provisions reflecting the homebuyer's detailed building requirements.

Before signing a construction contract, a buyer should obtain more than one estimate, which should describe in detail all work to be done, all costs and expected completion dates. Some contractors purposely make low bids that turn out to be more costly in the long run. Only hire a contractor who is licensed by local or state authorities and who has an established reputation. It is also a good idea to make sure your insurance coverage includes the new construction.

Once the terms are agreed upon, the buyer should obtain complete architectural plans and blueprints showing land, structures and internal layout, appliances, electrical and plumbing, material types and qualities and brand names to be used. These documents, which should be signed by the architect, contractor, and buyer, are an integral part of the contract of sale. Local ordinances should be checked to see if the plans conform to zoning and other applicable laws, although it is unlikely building permits will be issued unless they do. The contract of sale should also contain an agreed-upon procedure for the inevitable changes that occur, usually authorized only by written "change orders" signed by both the buyer and the contractor.

Since new houses are usually built on land sold by development or real estate companies or partnerships, the buyer must be sure to obtain a good and marketable title, as well as documentary proof that those selling the land own it unencumbered and have the legal authority to make the sale. Since unimproved lots are often mortgaged by the developer to finance the land purchase, the buyer should also be sure the developer/seller agrees to pay any existing mortgage. Before the final payment and settlement, a release of lien signed by the contractor and all subcontractors or suppliers should be obtained from the seller.

Financing for home building is customarily provided in installments contingent upon work completion. A lender will inspect work progress at various stages, before advancing the next cash installment to finance further work. All these terms will be spelled out in the installment construction mortgage agreed upon at the time of purchase. The builder's activity should be watched closely, so as not to hold up any financing due to unsatisfactory work.

Defects in newly installed appliances may be covered by manufacturer warranties, or they may be the responsibility of the builder if the defect is in installation. Complaints should always be in writing, in case the situation turns nasty and lawyers become involved. It is a good idea to withhold a portion of the contractor's final payment until everything is acceptable and in proper working order.

Misrepresentation by Seller

Until relatively recently, the rule of law covering real estate sales was caveat emptor, which is Latin for, "let the buyer beware." This rule placed a heavy obligation on a buyer to inspect the land and buildings before settlement and to ask every possible question about the conditions of both.

The only time a seller was held responsible for later discovered defects was when he or she (or the real estate broker) lied in response to the buyer's questions, or when defects were deliberately concealed from the buyer. Now, modern legal requirements hold the seller and broker liable for any negligent misrepresentations. Many states require brokers to personally inspect houses before they attempt to sell them, so they will have first-hand knowledge of the true condition, regardless of what the seller tells them.

It is absolutely essential that a buyer inspect the property, or better yet, hire a professional home and property inspection company to do the job. This assures the buyer of the true quality of the purchase and uncovers latent defects or problems.

Financing a Home Purchase

There are certain advantages to financing a home purchase, such as being able to deduct loan interest on personal income taxes. Financing should always be made a contingency in the sales contract so that if the buyer's good faith effort to obtain financing fails, the contract will terminate and the deposit will be returned.

Usually, home financing comes from a "conventional" or customary lender, such as a bank, mortgage company or savings and loan. But there are also various federal government programs available to qualified buyers, including the Federal Housing Administration (FHA) and the U.S. Department of Veterans Affairs (VA) home loan program. These government backed loans are often at reduced interest rates or with longer terms and include guarantees for conventional loans, as well as direct government loans.

In some cases, a buyer may be able to assume the existing mortgage of the seller, an attractive possibility if it has a lower interest rate. Whether it can be assumed often depends on the terms of the existing mortgage and usually requires the lender's approval. Often a seller will "take back a second mortgage," meaning he will loan the buyer the difference between available financing and the total asking price.

A *mortgage* is a document in which the buyer (the *mortgagor*) transfers an interest in the property to the lender (the *mortgagee*) as security for the amount loaned to finance the purchase. This security interest continues until the loan is paid in full, usually over a time period ranging from 10 to 30 years. In some areas, the preferred form of security document is a deed of trust, in which the lender's security interest is conveyed by the buyer to a third party, the trustee, until final payment. Both a mortgage and a *deed of trust* are accompanied by a *promissory note* signed by the buyer to the lender, stating the terms of the loan.

Under the federal law known as the Real Estate Settlement Procedures Act" (RESPA), at the time a loan application is submitted, a lender must provide a buyer with a complete statement describing his or her rights and all costs associated with the settlement, and costs and interest for the life of the mortgage. The Fair Housing Act of 1968 forbids discrimination in the sale or rental of housing based on race, color, religion, sex, national origin, handicap or families with children. A mortgage requires monthly payments from the buyer.

Failure to make payments eventually will result in the lender's seeking foreclosure of the mortgage, meaning the lender obtains a court order allowing the sale of the home unless the buyer pays up in full. The terms of every mortgage give lenders this right. Should the lender not obtain sufficient money at the sale to cover the total amount of the debt owed, plus legal and other foreclosure expenses, the errant buyer remains liable for the balance due and must vacate the property. Most state laws allow some form of redemption, meaning the buyer, even after foreclosure, has some limited time to redeem the property by paying all amounts due to the lender.

> **Comment:** *It is extremely important that you as a buyer who is acquiring financial liability under a mortgage understand thoroughly every term in the mortgage document. Mortgages are long and complicated, but you need to know about payment of real estate taxes if they are included, monthly payments and especially interest rates if they are subject to change. During the American housing market meltdown of 2007-2010, it became clear that thousands of banks and mortgage companies had offered, and millions of buyers had signed, easy money mortgages with future accelerated mortgage payments and interest rates, leading to massive foreclosures. U.S. household wealth fell by about $16.4 trillion of net worth from its peak in spring 2007, about six months before the start of the recession, to when things hit bottom in the first quarter of 2009, according to figures from the Federal Reserve. Before you sign, be sure you understand what could happen in the future and assume the worst.*

The Homebuyers Title

Every buyer must obtain what is known as a *marketable title*, meaning a title free from any defects. In order to assure a marketable title, either the buyer's attorney or a title company (or both) may have a hand in examining public records to be sure there are no title defects. If a title company is willing to issue a title insurance policy, which guarantees payment of any future costs in defending the title, you can be reasonably sure the title is good. Be careful when obtaining title insurance that it covers you as the buyer, since many times it is required by the financing lender and only covers the lender.

The transfer of ownership of real estate is accomplished by a formal document signed by the seller known as a *deed* that must contain an accurate description of the location, boundaries and total area of the property being conveyed.

There are several types of deeds, some containing greater guarantees than others. A *general warranty deed* guarantees the seller has a marketable title and there are no encumbrances. A *full warranty deed* guarantees the same and also promises the seller will clear up any future title questions which may arise. A *quitclaim deed* is nothing more than a transfer of any interest the seller may have in the property, if any at all does exist. Whatever form the deed takes, it should be recorded in the appropriate public land records just as soon as the settlement occurs.

There are several different estates, or degrees of interests in land which an owner can obtain. The interest with the greatest extent of control is known as a *fee simple absolute*, a phrase which appears in the deed, meaning complete and unrestricted ownership, and the right to convey title as the owner wishes. A person may also obtain a *life estate*, literally meaning the right to live on and use the land during the owner's life, or the life of another, at the end of which, the land passes to other persons. A life estate is often created by a last will when one spouse leaves property to the surviving spouse for life, then to their children. The children who will eventually receive the property are said to have a *future interest*.

There are also certain modern forms of property ownership reflecting changing trends in land use. A *condominium* is one unit in a multiple unit building, which is conveyed by a deed granting ownership of the described area of space within that unit, together with right to use common areas of the entire development such as halls, garage and parking space, a swimming pool and other facilities. In a *cooperative* (or co-op), land and buildings are owned by a corporation with individual unit residents as shareholders who lease their apartments. In a time share arrangement, multiple owners by contract purchase an undivided interest in vacation property, which they may use for specific time periods each year.

Restrictions on Property

Notwithstanding the fact that an owner has the theoretical right to the free and unfettered use and enjoyment of his real property, there are various restrictions that may be imposed by written provisions in the deed conveying title or imposed by law.

Deeds often contain *restrictive covenants* preventing certain described uses of the property, such as forbidding the use of a residence as an office or the keeping of animals. The most common restrictions are setbacks, governing the distance placement of buildings or building additions in relation to the property boundaries. Be sure to obtain a copy of the land records before final settlement and understand how restrictions affect your land use.

Easements on the property are limited rights granted to others for certain purposes to enter or use the property, such as electric or telephone utilities erecting and maintaining a pole or other equipment, or the use of a road to reach an adjacent property. Easements usually continue to exist even though ownership of the property changes.

A slightly unusual form of potential land restriction is allowed under the *doctrine of adverse possession*. This occurs when a person openly and continuously uses or occupies another person's land for a period of time — varying from five to 20 years, depending on state law. This possession must be "hostile," meaning the occupier claims ownership. Admittedly this is more of a problem in rural areas where someone builds a cabin in a remote corner of a vast tract of land, but it can also occur when an unsettled boundary or an unauthorized road goes unchallenged for the required number years.

If there is *surface water* on your land (a creek, a stream, or run off after heavy rain), in some states an owner has no right to divert the natural flow so as to harm neighbors. Other states allow an owner to deal with water flows in any way that protects him or her, viewing it as a common enemy of everyone in the area.

In eastern states, there is generally no right to permanently divert large quantities of water so as to short change others using the same river or stream as a water source. In western states, where water is scarce, the law allows a "first come, first-served" approach, so that late arrivals cannot interfere with prior existing water uses.

Though it is less used these days with most public infrastructure already in place, federal, state, and local governments have the *power of eminent domain*, allowing the taking of private property (with "just compensation" to the owners) for public purposes such as a highway, school, park or sewer construction. If the government and the owner cannot agree on a fair price, the government can go to court and seek condemnation proceedings, forcing the sale to the state.

Chapter 7

Perhaps one of the toughest controls government imposes on land is *zoning*, the restriction of every parcel of land to a certain limited use or uses, such as residential or commercial activity.

In addition, there are various state land use laws which now impose restrictions, such as no building on (or disturbance of) wetlands or other environmentally fragile areas, or no building within certain distances from waterfront areas.

There are also local fire and safety building codes that must be adhered to, especially in new or refurbishing construction. For example, because of the spread of home building into previously unsettled arid and semi-desert areas of the West, many local codes require all roofs to have non-wood or fire retardant materials to prevent destruction by forest or brush wildfires.

Before you agree to purchase real property, you should be aware of all the potential restrictions that may apply to the use of the land.

> **Comment:** *The purchase of a home (or any real estate) is a major financial commitment obligating the buyer for years to come. With the huge number of potential legal and physical problems associated with real estate and its acquisition, it is best for the parties (especially the buyer) to be represented by an attorney. Having an attorney is not so important for a buyer if the title is to be examined and insured by an established title company, which assumes many of the functions of the lawyer. But keep in mind that the real estate agent representing the seller is doing just that — making a sale. In some areas, it is customary for the seller's agent to act as agent for the buyer as well, presenting a potential conflict of interest. Unless you are experienced in real estate transactions, you should consult a lawyer before you sign a contract of sale.*

Environmental Law

Although they apply to all real property, environmental laws usually have more application to commercial properties, especially those engaged in manufacturing and other processes which may emit pollutants of various kinds. In the last 30 years, numerous federal and state laws have been adopted, holding property owners responsible for activities on their land which despoil the air, water or earth, or injure the health or wellbeing of people, wildlife or vegetation.

At the federal level, these laws, most administered by the U.S. Environmental Protection Agency (EPA), include protection against water pollution (especially of drinking water sources), preservation of coastal areas and wetlands, the location and cleanup of toxic and hazardous substances, protection for endangered species of wildlife and marine mammals, commercial fishery limitations and the Clean Air Act of 1990.

It is necessary to understand that these federal and state environmental laws may well impact on your use and enjoyment of any land you purchase. For example, in certain areas of the Chesapeake Bay in Maryland and Virginia, waterfront home owners could be in technical violation of the law if they mow their lawns immediately adjacent to wetlands areas because the mean high tide mark and the type of vegetation growing in such areas may cause it to be included in protected wetlands.

Even though real estate agents should make known to prospective buyers all environmental restrictions on property they offer for sale, buyers should always investigate independently.

2. Landlord and Tenant Law

With the average median purchase price of a residential single family home in the United States just under $212,000 in 2015, the dream of home ownership is beyond the reach of a great many Americans. Renting an apartment, house, condo or other dwelling is the only alternative for many.

Landlord-tenant law covers a web of legal interaction between rental property owners (known as *lessors* or *landlords*) and renters (known as *lessees* or *tenants*). The contract which transfers from the landlord to the tenant the right to possession of real estate in exchange for the periodic payment of rent for a stated period of time is the lease.

A *periodic tenancy* is a verbal lease, usually for a weekly or monthly occupancy. Notice to terminate by either party must be for the length of the periodic lease. A lease for a year or more is a *tenancy for years*, and about 40 states have laws requiring such leases to be in writing to be effective.

Whatever the length of a lease, it is best for the tenant to "get it in writing" so there is no question about the rights of both parties. The lease should state when, where and to whom rent is payable. It should detail who is responsible for paying for utilities and repairs, and whether you are to receive credit for repairs you make yourself. Check to see if pets are allowed. Most leases prohibit a tenant from assigning or "subleasing" without permission of the landlord. (See sample on next page.)

Most leases for a term of a year or more require the tenant to pay a security deposit which, depending on state law, can equal up to three months' rent. Usually this amount will pay for the first and last month's rent, plus a one-month rental amount as security for damages, refundable when you leave.

When the lease ends, either the landlord or tenant must give 30 days' notice of intent not to renew the rental. If the tenant remains without a new lease, this becomes a periodic tenancy. A tenant who abandons a rental unit before the lease expires remains liable for the unpaid rent to the end of the lease, unless the landlord signifies acceptance of the abandonment in writing or by re-renting the unit.

A landlord has a right to evict a tenant before the lease ends for a limited number of causes, such as the tenant engaging in illegal conduct on the premises or failure to pay rent. In almost all states, the law now requires a landlord to give formal notice to a tenant to vacate, unless he or she pays back rent within a specified number of days. (See sample on page 132.)

Failure to pay allows the landlord to go to court to seek eviction in a summary proceeding. This requires several days, and a notice will be given to the tenant of the court hearing date. This allows the tenant a chance to pay back rent and other expenses to avoid eviction. Unless a state law allows it, a landlord has no right to retain personal property of a tenant as security for payment of back rent.

Commercial leases usually do not have as many protections for business tenants as do residential leases. This is because business tenants often make substantial alterations to the premises and assume all obligations for repairs and maintenance.

While it is rarely necessary to consult an attorney before signing a lease, it is very important to read every clause so you understand exactly what your obligation will be. Remember, printed leases always favor the landlord, so judge the terms accordingly.

Residential Lease Agreement

LEASE AGREEMENT, entered into by and between *property owner's name* ('Landlord') and *renter's name* ('Tenant'). For good and valuable consideration the parties agree as follows:

1. Landlord hereby leases and lets to Tenant the premises described as follows: *address of rental property*

2. This lease shall be for a term of *length of lease* beginning on *date lease begins*, 20__, and ending on *date lease ends*, 20__.

3. Tenant shall pay Landlord rent in the amount of $ *amount of rent* per month during said term, payable on the *day rent is due* day of each month in advance. Tenant shall pay Landlord a security deposit of $*amount of deposit*, to be returned upon termination of this Lease and the payment of all rents due and performance of all other obligations.

4. Tenant shall at his/her own expense provide the following utilities or services: *list utilities and services tenant must pay for in addition to rent.* Landlord shall at his/her expense provide the following utilities or services: *list utilities and services landlord must pay for.*

5. Tenant further agrees that:

a) Upon the expiration of the Lease, Tenant shall return possession of the leased premises to Landlord in its present condition, except for reasonable wear and tear. Tenant shall commit no waste to the leased premises.

b) Tenant shall not assign or sublet the premises or allow any other person to occupy the leased premises without Landlord's prior written consent.

c) Tenant shall not make any material or structural alterations to the leased premises or change locks on the premises without Landlord's prior written consent.

d) Tenant shall comply with all building, zoning, and health codes and other applicable laws for the use of said leased premises.

e) Tenant shall not conduct on premises any activity deemed by Landlord hazardous, a nuisance, or requiring an increase in fire or hazard insurance premiums.

f) Tenant shall not allow pets on the premises without the prior written consent of the Landlord.

g) In the event of any breach of the payment of rent, or any other breach of this Lease, Landlord shall have full rights to terminate this Lease in accordance with state law and re-enter and reclaim possession of the leased premises, in addition to such other remedies which are available to Landlord as a result of said breach.

6. This Lease shall be binding upon and inure to the benefit of the parties, their successors, agents, assigns, and personal representatives.

7. This Lease shall be subordinate to all present or future mortgages against the property.

8. Additional Lease terms: _____

Signed this date day of month, 20 _

Witness' signature	*Landlord's' signature*
Witness	Landlord
Witness' signature	*Tenant's signature*
Witness	Tenant

It is best to put a lease agreement in writing so there is no question about the rights of both parties.

Chapter 7

In most states, the law requires that a landlord give notice to a tenant to vacate, unless the overdue rent is paid within a specified number of days.

In most states, the law requires that a landlord give notice to a tenant to vacate, unless the overdue rent is paid within a specified number of days.

Landlord's Notice to Vacate

[SEND CERTIFIED MAIL — RETURN RECEIPT REQUESTED]

Date: _____

To: *tenant's name and address*

and all others now in possession of the premises described below:

You are hereby notified to quit, vacate, and deliver possession of the premises you hold as our tenant, namely *address of rental property* on or before *date*, 20_

This notice is provided due to nonpayment of rent. The present rent arrearage is in the amount of $ *amount of overdue rent*.

You may redeem your tenancy by full payment of this amount on or before *date*, 20___. Should you fail to bring your rent payments current or, in the alternative, vacate the premises, I will immediately take legal action as the law requires to evict you and to recover such rents and damages for the unlawful detention of the premises as are permitted by law.

Landlord's signature _____

Landlord

---

3. Personal Property Law

Although this book touches upon many aspects of law governing the ownership, use and transfer of personal property, there are a few points that need discussion because they arise in daily activities involving such property.

Bailments

A *bailment* is the delivery of property by its owner (the *bailor*) to another person (the *bailee*) for some specific purpose, after the accomplishment of which, the property is returned to the owner. Leaving a dress or suit at the cleaners or a car at the repair shop are examples of this type of activity. A bailment differs from a sale because ownership is not transferred from one party to another. It is different from a loan because a loan terminates at a set time. It's different from a "chattel" or personal property mortgage, because no lender is involved and no equitable interest created in a bailment.

A bailee is liable for negligent damage to the property and must use reasonable care and diligence while the property is in his possession. A bailee may limit his liability by agreement, (so read the fine print on the back of the laundry ticket).

There are certain types of semi-intangible personal property, sometimes called *intellectual property*, ownership of which the law protects. This property includes the right to someone's intellectual property. Such things as the thoughts and words contained in books, newspaper or magazine articles, movies, television or stage screenplays, poems, music and songs with lyrics, video games, computer software programs, cassette tapes, records, CDs, photographs, drawings, paintings, maps, catalogs, dance routines. The list is endless, but they all have in common an original source inside someone's brain.

Copyrights

In order to establish a copyright, the author only needs to display on copies of the work, in whatever form it is produced, a written notice such as "Copyright 2015, Robert E. Bauman" or the symbol and name "© 2015, Robert E. Bauman." This protects the work against copying, reproduction, or use by anyone without the author's permission.

In order for a copyright owner to be able to sue for damages against those that use the copyrighted material without proper permission, the Copyright Act of 1976 requires a person who creates or produces such property to register his or her ownership with the Copyright Office in Washington, D.C. This can be done by sending in a copyright form, two copies of the work to be registered and protected, and a small fee.

For works made for hire and anonymous works, the duration of copyright is 95 years from first publication, or 120 years from creation, whichever is shorter, unless the author's identity is later revealed in Copyright Office records, in which case the term becomes the author's life plus 70 years.

A copyright owner can sell or transfer this property interest as he or she pleases. It is not a violation of copyright, but rather is known in law as fair use when another person uses copyrighted material in news reporting, critical reviews, comment, teaching or research. A copyright owner can sue if infringement occurs, obtaining actual damages and an injunction against further misuse.

Chapter 7

Domestic American copyright law is augmented by international copyright treaties (known as "conventions"), which extend protection throughout all countries that are parties to these agreements.

Patents & Trademarks

Property rights are created and can be protected by law when a person who is the original inventor creates a unique product, manufacturing or other process, a machine, chemical or other compounds of matter or an original design for some object. As a rule, the subject of the patent must be capable of being carried out in some way, and should have some actual "utility."

A patent granted for an invention lasts for 20 years and 14 years for a design.

Patents (and commercial trademarks) are granted by the U.S. Patent and Trademark Office, located in Arlington, Virginia, part of the U.S. Department of Commerce. In order to protect your patent rights, you must apply for registration soon after the invention is completed. If you market the product and do not apply, you could lose the right to a patent. Legal protection begins as soon as the patent application is filed. As with copyright violations, patent holders can sue for damages if others misappropriate their products or ideas without permission.

A *trademark*™ is a distinctive mark, symbol or device a manufacturer affixes to a product to identify it for the buying public. A trademark differs from a trade name. The words "Coca Cola" are a trade name, but the distinctive cursive script in which that trade name has been printed for many years, is a trademark. Trademarks are also protected by statute and at common law.

Commercial Paper

As you might imagine, there is a substantial body of law governing the creation, transfer and ownership of what is called commercial paper or *negotiable instruments* (checks drawn on banks, drafts, promissory notes and other papers which are not cash, but are accepted as legal payment of money). Such non-cash payment transactions are governed by the Uniform Commercial Code (UCC), which is law in all states and now extends to electronic transfers of money as well.

This area of law is primarily of interest to bankers, brokers, investors, their lawyers, and to governments concerned with currency flows and money laundering. Most people are touched by negotiable instruments law when writing a personal or business bank check, which the UCC defines as "a draft drawn on a bank and payable on demand." Checks must be cashed within a reasonable period of time, 30 days or less and banks are obligated by law to credit bank deposits of checks within three to five days, depending on the geographic location of the domestic bank on which the check is drawn. This area of the law is very complex and may require an attorney's counsel.

Chapter 8:
Transportation Law

This chapter addresses the impact of the law on automobiles and how you can best avoid the problems that go with owning and operating a motor vehicle. It also discusses admiralty law (the rules governing ships and navigation on rivers, lakes and other bodies of water) and aviation law.

1. Motor Vehicles

State motor vehicle codes require several volumes to catalog all the laws governing police traffic control and vehicle sale and registration. Many volumes of the United States Code (U.S.C.) govern the construction and use of interstate highways, motor transport, maximum speed limits, highway "beautification" and pollution emission controls imposed on manufacturers of motor vehicles.

Although state law governs most motor vehicle matters, the U.S. Congress forces states to comply with federal policy by withholding highway construction and other transportation funds unless state law conforms to what Washington politicians want.

Drivers Licenses

Every state requires drivers to have an official motor vehicle operator's license, renewable every few years. There are several classes of driver's licenses matched to each type of vehicle operated — automobiles, trucks of various sizes, buses, emergency vehicles, etc.

You can lose your license if you are convicted of driving while drunk or on drugs, if you refuse to take a blood alcohol test when stopped by police, if you fail to maintain auto insurance coverage, or if you accumulate more than a maximum number of "points" for moving violations within a certain time period.

Unreal ID

The so-called "Real I.D. Act of 2005" is a U.S. federal law that imposes security, authentication and issuance standards for

American state driver's licenses and state ID cards. It is one of the best examples of Big Brother government mentality.

Anyone who has ever stood in line at a state motor vehicles agency would know better, but the U.S. Congress foolishly assigned the control and administration of this monstrous new program to just those bureaucratic agencies. The law federalizes and standardizes state driver's licenses for all 50 states, and it will result in something that has been resisted in this country for a long time — a de facto national identity card.

And if you don't have the new ID card that the Act requires, you won't be able to board commercially operated airline flights or entering federal buildings, although the U.S. Department of Homeland Security (DHS) said that this will not be implemented before January 1, 2016.

The Real I.D. Act would impose numerous new burdens on taxpayers, citizens, immigrants and state governments — while doing nothing to protect against terrorism. As a result, the law has caused intense opposition from many groups across the political spectrum, but to no avail. The first stages of the law took effect in 2008. As of April 2015, 23 states and territories are compliant, 27 states and territories have been granted renewable extensions, and 6 states and territories are noncompliant.

Accidents

Billions of miles traveled each year produce hundreds of thousands of automobile accidents — and thousands of lawsuits seeking millions of dollars in compensation for property damage, personal injury and wrongful death.

A driver has a duty to operate a motor vehicle in the careful manner that an ordinarily reasonable and prudent person would employ under similar circumstances. This includes taking into account road and weather conditions and keeping alert for dangers. It also means a greater degree of care when driving in the presence of pedestrians or children. Violations of this standard of reasonable care will make a driver liable for consequential damages.

As a general rule, a driver has the right of way traveling between one street or road intersection and the next, and a pedestrian on foot has the right of way at an intersection.

In a few states, in order for a passenger injured in an auto accident to recover damages against the driver, there must be a showing of *gross negligence* on the part of the driver, a serious breach of duty such as driving while intoxicated, or a showing of reckless disregard for the consequences. Many states allow injured passengers to prove a driver's negligence under the ordinary tort rules measuring such acts.

If a motor vehicle owner allows a person to drive his or her vehicle while knowing the person to be a reckless driver, or, in some states, if the owner gives permission to any driver, the law will hold the owner liable for any resulting damage under the rule of *imputed negligence*. Similarly, if a negligent employee causes injury while driving a vehicle in the course of his or her employment, the employer will be held liable.

In 20 states, the *family purpose doctrine* holds both the owner of the car and the driver liable for damages caused by any family member when driving for family use. Thirty-eight states have "*dram shop*" laws holding the seller of alcoholic beverages liable for any injury caused by a person to whom alcohol is sold when the buyer was obviously intoxicated. Several states have extended this liability to private persons who provide alcohol to an intoxicated guest who later causes injury to others.

As with other types of negligence, in order for an injured party to prove liability in an auto accident, the accused defendant's negligence must be shown to be the proximate cause of the injury, defined as any injury-producing act or omission having the likely (and therefore, foreseeable) result of causing such injury.

The negligent act need not be the direct or immediate cause of the injury in order to be "proximate" and impose liability, so long as the act is the efficient cause ("efficient" in the sense of "cause and effect"), and there is no intervening cause between that act and the ultimate injury. Thus, one can be liable for negligence because of an original act setting in motion a chain of events which, when combined, causes injury.

In Alabama, North Carolina, Tennessee, Virginia, Maryland and the District of Columbia, if the plaintiff (the individual claiming the injury) is guilty of contributory negligence, the defendant will not be liable. A driver's liability may be lessened by the *rule of comparative negligence*, a situation in which both parties are wrong, and fault is apportioned. Also, under the *doctrine of last clear chance*, a contributory negligent driver can hold the other driver liable if that party had the opportunity, yet failed to avoid the accident.

The *personal injury damages* for which a negligent motor vehicle operator can be held liable include medical expenses, lost wages, pain and suffering, disability and wrongful death. *Property damages* are usually limited to repair costs or the "book value" of the car (if not repairable), plus temporary auto rental. "Book value" is the worth assigned to a vehicle based on its year of manufacture and model.

When You are in an Accident

If you are involved in a collision, the first thing to do is stop. Never leave the scene of an accident, or you could be guilty of a "hit and run" criminal felony, far more serious in its legal consequences than the accident itself.

If anyone is injured, get medical help as quickly as possible. Notify the police. Failure to report an accident is usually a crime. Get all the information about the other driver and vehicle that you can — name, license plate number, make, model, insurance company, names of passengers, witnesses, etc. Give the same information to the other party. Never admit guilt or liability on your part.

> **Comment:** *If you or anyone else has suffered serious bodily injury, you should consult with a good personal injury lawyer as soon as possible. Never sign any papers presented by your insurance company or that of the other party without a lawyer reviewing them first. It is customary for insurance company agents to move in fast and try to limit their liability. Don't be in a hurry to settle. Most states allow the filing of lawsuits for a year (or even several years) after an accident occurs, and often injuries are not fully known for months after the event.*

Drunk Driving

It is a criminal offense in every state to operate a motor vehicle while your mental or physical abilities are "impaired" by alcohol or other drugs. Variously known as DUI ("driving under the influence") or DWI ("driving while intoxicated"), this offense covers not only alcoholic intoxication, but also impairment resulting from the use of illegal drugs ("controlled dangerous substances"), such as cocaine or marijuana, as well as legal prescription drugs.

In recent years, the penalties for DUI offenses have been increased considerably, even for first offenders, often requiring mandatory time in jail. These laws have also lowered the permissible blood alcohol content as a measurement of a driver's drunkenness. In some states, a measurement of 0.10 percent (meaning two drinks within 60 minutes) could place a driver in the danger zone.

Police officers have the right to stop and test you for drunkenness if you are driving erratically or if they smell booze after a routine traffic stop. In some states, if you refuse to take a portable "Breathalyzer" test, your driver's license can be revoked.

Possible DUI Defenses

Attorneys specializing in DUI cases look for technicalities to avoid going to trial, where the outcome may be a lot worse than paying a fine and not contesting the charges. Here are some of the most common DUI defenses:

- Incorrect police paperwork, such as a wrong date or an incorrect driver's license number.
- Laws (in some states) that forbid arrests for drunk driving made on private property.
- Lack of independent proof that the charged individual is, in fact, the one who was driving the vehicle. (For example, the police officer may have arrived at the scene after everyone had already exited the vehicle.)
- Lack of territorial jurisdiction. (An officer can make an arrest outside his or her jurisdiction only when a pursuit of the suspect was involved.)
- Involuntary intoxication. (For instance, if it can be proved that someone spiked your fruit punch with an intoxicating substance.)
- Necessity. (For instance, if a drunken individual pulls over to the side of the road and falls asleep, but is awakened by a threatening man with a gun, driving away may be necessary.)

If the officer conducts a field test and judges you to be drunk, he can take you to a testing facility, where breath, blood and/

or urine tests may be taken. Some states permit these tests to be done without consent.

Comment: If you are charged with a DUI offense, obtain the services of a lawyer immediately. With increased penalties and strong public opposition to drunk driving, this is not a matter to be taken lightly.

Fighting Traffic Tickets

In nearly every traffic violation case, when the question is whether to believe the police or the driver, a judge will most certainly side with the police. Unless the driver can show concrete evidence, produce a disinterested witness or successfully question the accuracy of the police radar calibration — he or she won't have much of a chance.

If you have received a moving violation, be sure to follow the instructions on the back of the ticket to the letter. You may be lucky — the police officer might not appear in court, in which case you should ask that the case be dismissed.

If you are stopped for speeding, be totally cooperative and never do anything that may make you memorable to the police officer.

Comment: In some cases, it could cost you more to hire a lawyer than it would to pay the fine. But, if your driving record is a mess, or your cumulative points against license revocation is about to max out, it will probably be worth it to have an attorney represent you. In major cities there are law firms that specialize in traffic ticket cases and they often have established very good rapport with the judges who hear such cases. Find out which firm has the best track record.

Auto Insurance

In 31 states, a person injured in an auto accident can recover damages from the person responsible under general rules of tort liability. In most cases, an auto insurance company pays the damages to the injured party on behalf of its insured driver who was held liable.

All states impose "minimum auto insurance coverage" requirements for bodily injury and property damage, although you can purchase greater coverage. "Collision coverage" pays for physical damage to your car, and "comprehensive coverage" pays for events like a stolen stereo, or water and wind damage. "Uninsured motorist coverage" pays if you are hit by someone who has no insurance.

Nineteen states have adopted "no-fault" auto insurance laws, under which an injured party is paid for economic losses (medical expenses and lost wages) by his own insurance company, but is limited in seeking any other damages against the negligent party. Each state no-fault law differs, and an insurance agent can explain local applications of the law.

Most states have an "uninsured motorist fund," into which drivers unable to obtain coverage are obliged to pay amounts based on their driving records, before they can register or be licensed to operate a motor vehicle. These state funds are a payment source for damages caused by uninsured motorists.

Buying a Car

Under federal law, each new vehicle must have attached to it a "sticker" outlining the suggested manufacturer's retail price for the model, plus the costs of all optional equipment and accessories. The total "sticker price" is usually the starting point for negotiating.

Auto purchases can be financed either by a bank, usually with better terms, or by the auto dealer under the company's finance plan, often with larger down payments and shorter pay out time.

An auto purchase contract is like any other contract, there must be an offer to buy the car, an acceptance of the offer by the dealer and "consideration" (something of value, like money, paid by the buyer in return for the car). The contract should specifically identify the car by its serial number, name all accessories and state the purchase price, payment terms and all warranties.

A manufacturer's warranty usually guarantees the workmanship and parts against defects, the power train and rust protection, each for a described period of time and total number. This is an express warranty and is limited by its wording. Any specific warranty about the vehicle must be added in writing to be effective. All states have laws requiring a seller generally to guarantee a new car's warranty of merchantability, meaning its condition allows it to be safely operated on public streets and highways.

Two thirds of the states and Washington, D.C., now have so-called *lemon laws*, applying to vehicles that turn out to have major defects. These laws differ somewhat, but most require a manufacturer to replace a new car or refund the purchase price if a major defect has not been repaired after four times in the shop (or a cumulative 30 days of repair work in the shop), or after failure to repair during the first 12,000 miles of operation.

There is also a general right under the Magnuson-Moss Act, a federal law, for any purchaser of a consumer product, including autos, to sue in state court for a breach of an express or implied product warranty. When buying a used car, the old rule of "let the buyer beware" still applies for the most part. Sellers have little more than an obligation to warrant that the car is safe to operate in public, although federal law does require a "sticker" stating any warranties, or whether the car is sold "as is."

The sale of a motor vehicle implies that the seller, either a dealer or a private person, has a valid title which can be transferred, usually evidenced by a state department of motor vehicles certificate. It is also legally implied that the vehicle is not encumbered by any liens or other security interest, a fact usually shown on the title certificate. A state motor vehicle agency will not transfer title until it receives proof a lien has been paid. If a car has been stolen, a subsequent purchaser ignorant of that fact cannot obtain good title.

The owner of a motor vehicle is legally required to maintain it in a condition allowing safe operation. Failure to keep the car in good condition can subject the owner to police citations for each violation. Although one of the leading national consumer complaints is about getting ripped off by auto repair businesses, few states have any comprehensive laws regulating their conduct. This means that unless you personally know the repair shop and the quality of its work, you should get a written estimate of costs, parts needed, time required, and any warranty on the outcome before authorizing any work on your car.

Whether from a finance company or a bank, when an automobile loan is obtained, the lender usually retains a security interest in the car until the loan is paid in full. This is called a *secured loan*, the lender's retained title serving as the security. In either case, the lender has the right to repossess the car if the buyer is in *default*, meaning he or she can take back the car if agreed payments have not been made. In some agreements, default occurs when the buyer fails to maintain insurance on the vehicle.

Some states require the lender to notify the buyer that he or she is in default before repossession can be attempted, and some allow the buyer a chance to "cure" the default by immediate payment. Other states require no notice. Most reputable lenders will give notice simply because obtaining a last chance payment is far less trouble and far less expensive than physical repossession of a vehicle.

The main legal limitation on a secured creditor's right to repossess an auto is a prohibition against causing a *breach of the peace*, meaning any physical or violent confrontation that might produce personal injury. Some state laws specifically bar a "repo man" from breaking into a person's garage or home, and a few forbid breaking into a locked car. Most states do not permit the car buyer to use force to stop repossession. Some states allow the delinquent buyer to cure the default after repossession, but a buyer better move quickly, because a lender is likely to sell the car right away to a more reliable purchaser.

2. Waterborne Transportation

Admiralty law is the branch of law governing waterborne travel and commerce on oceans, coastal waters and all navigable waters within the United States, including bays, canals, rivers and lakes. Admiralty also covers maritime contracts, vessels of all kinds and injuries to people and property occurring on water.

Admiralty law is, in theory, the joint legal province of both the states and the federal government. But as a practical matter, most admiralty cases are heard in U.S. district courts, where judges specializing in such matters apply special admiralty rules. These courts can enforce a lien against a vessel and have jurisdiction over all privately owned vessels.

Repossession

Chapter 8

Ship owners can be held strictly liable for personal injury to crew members or passengers, if the ship is proven to be "unseaworthy" and that condition causes injury or death. Federal law governs vessel safety, health and operational standards, and the U.S. Coast Guard is usually the enforcement agency involved.

Generally, a ship owner's liability for lost or damaged cargo is limited to the value of the vessel, and in the case of individual passengers, the previously declared value of personal property.

If a person voluntarily goes to the rescue of a ship, its crew or its cargo, the *law of salvage* allows compensation for such heroic efforts. If a ship is abandoned by its captain and crew it becomes the property of whoever is able to salvage it.

As in the case of motor vehicles on land, state law requires annual registration of all vessels over a certain size and payment of an annual fee. Some states are now considering laws to require a boat operator's license for small craft (larger vessel operators must pass Coast Guard tests), because of the increasing number of accidents on crowded waterways due to alcohol and drugs.

> **Comment:** *Admiralty law and procedure is one of the most esoteric areas of law. It has changed little since the days of British naval dominance of the world's oceans. The number of lawyers who practice admiralty law is very limited. If you have a serious admiralty law problem, hire a lawyer who shows you a certificate of membership in the admiralty bar and check his or her references.*

3. Aviation Law

Most of the law applying to aviation is federal in nature. If you want to qualify as a private pilot, you must complete specified training courses for various types of aircraft before the Federal Aviation Administration (FAA) will issue you a license. Certain "flying schools" are FAA-approved and can certify your training once you qualify. Commercial pilot licenses are more difficult to obtain, but also come from the FAA.

Under Federal law, lost luggage liability for domestic air carriers is limited to $750, and for international flights, about €1,300 (euros) per kilo of checked baggage (which at this writing equals about US$1,600). Lost or damaged baggage and contents are reimbursed at their current value. If a person is injured or killed on an international flight stopping in, originating in or destined for the United States, under the "Montreal Convention" (an international air liability treaty), the maximum recovery is $130,000. But this limited amount is only recoverable if notice of limitation is prominently displayed in writing on your ticket or other air travel document. If notice is not given, a greater recovery may be possible. You can bet almost all tickets have the notice.

If you are "bumped" from an overbooked flight, you are entitled to a seat on the next available flight or a full refund. If you lose a big business deal because of this situation, you probably will have to sue if you want compensatory damages.

Chapter 8

CHAPTER 9:
CONTRACTS AND CONSUMER LAW

1. The Law of Contracts

The word *contract* comes from the Latin *contractus*, meaning, "to draw together." In law, a contract is a binding agreement between two or more persons — a promise made between parties creating a mutual obligation.

In order to be valid and enforceable, a contract must include *legal capacity*, *an offer*, *an acceptance* and *valid consideration*. There must be at least two parties to a contract, and the agreement must be complete in its terms (containing definite obligations of each party, including the time, place, and method to be used in accomplishing the agreement).

Legal capacity means that the parties of the contract must be at least 18 years of age. (A minor who is a party to a contract is not obliged to carry it out.) In addition, parties must have mental ability sufficient to understand the contract and cannot be impaired by alcohol or drugs. If a party to a contract is acting as an agent for another person (a principal), the agent's authority should be in writing.

An *offer* is a promise by one person (the *offeror*) to another person (the *offeree*) to do or not to do some designated act in the future. There must be a definite and clear promise; an expression of mere intent is not sufficient as an offer.

To be valid, an offer must be definite in its terms concerning time, place of performance and other material factors. An offer can be withdrawn by an unambiguous revocation any time before it is accepted. An offer can also be ended by rejection, lapse of time attached to the acceptance, the occurrence of any contingency attached to the offer, death of one of the essential parties or destruction of the subject matter.

An *acceptance* of an offer sufficient to form a contract can be done orally or by conduct stipulated in the offer. If the offer describes a specific means of acceptance, a contract exists only once that is done. For example, if a written offer stipulates the acceptance is to be "in writing and hand-delivered," and the offeree faxes the letter instead, the offeror has the option of refusing the acceptance.

A *counteroffer* is considered to be a new offer and not an acceptance. Unless it states a time, an acceptance may be made within a "reasonable time," usually 30 days. Common sense decides what is "reasonable" under the circumstances.

Consideration (giving up something in return for something else) is also required for a valid contract. The law in many states now presumes all written contracts to have valid consideration, unless otherwise proven. In most cases, consideration involves monetary value, but a money exchange is not necessary to make a contract valid. It is also unnecessary for the person making the promise to receive benefit in order for consideration to be valid.

When a person promises to do something, he or she is obligated to fulfill his or her part of the contract on the *theory of promissory estoppel*, which means that one party cannot renege on an agreement causing detriment to the other party. Under most circumstances, once a contract is agreed to, its terms can be changed only by mutual agreement of both parties. A contract which has an objective that is illegal or against public policy is not legally enforceable.

Contracts Required to be in Writing

Since certain types of contracts are especially susceptible to fraud, all states and the District of Columbia now require that the following contracts be in writing in order to be enforceable in court:

- Contracts concerning real estate (except leases of less than one year)

- Lifetime contracts or contracts impossible to perform in less than one year

- Contracts for goods costing $500 or more (but even if a contract over $500 is oral, once the goods are received, the contract becomes enforceable)

- Contracts based on consideration of marriage, such as pre-marital and property settlement agreements; and

• A promise to pay another person's debts

A contract is *breached* when a party fails to perform (either entirely or partially) the contractual obligations, without justification for the failure.

If the breach on the part of one party is minor, the other party still must carry out his or her obligations, but may be entitled to compensation for any damage the breach causes.

Breach of Contract

When a contract is breached, the injured party can sue for breach of contract seeking these remedies:

• Payment of *compensatory money damages*; and/or,

• *Specific performance*, in which the court orders the party at fault to carry out the contract terms under possible punishment for contempt of court. This remedy is available only when money damages clearly would not be sufficient, as when a seller of land attempts to back out of the sale. Specific performance is not granted when personal services are involved because of the 13th Amendment's constitutional prohibition against slavery and forced servitude. But a court might order the breaching party not to perform similar services for the injured party's competitors during the life of the contract.

If a person is induced to agree to a contract by *fraud*, he or she can sue to cancel the contract, seek money damages and also sue the other party for the tort of fraud.

When both parties decide to cancel or *rescind* a contract, each must return whatever he or she has received, so that both parties are made whole. If a disagreement arises over the meaning of the contract, and you compromise, it is an *accord* and *satisfaction*.

Because there is a presumption that unsolicited door-to-door sales made in the home often involve "high pressure" sales tactics, federal rules allow anyone making a purchase in such a situation the absolute right to cancel the contract within three calendar days.

Years ago, many states had laws that allowed an injured party to sue for damages for *breach of promise to marry* when the other party backed out. These laws have all been repealed.

Contract Interpretation

When the terms of a contract are disputed by the parties, a court looks not to the individual words, sentences, paragraphs and clauses, but to the overall meaning of the contract and the intention of the parties. Words are given their ordinary definition unless they have a technical meaning, and trade customs bearing on the meaning may be examined. Any doubts are resolved against the party who actually prepared the document.

The *parole evidence rule* generally prevents a court from considering any oral testimony or previous verbal agreements in order to interpret a current contract. Parole evidence is usually allowed if there is ambiguity, or to show fraud, duress, mistake or lack of consideration.

> **Comment:** *Most everyday contracts are oral and hardly require the advice of an attorney — just your careful consideration and a mutual understanding between the parties. If the proposed contract is to be in writing (indicating its importance) and you have any questions about the true meaning, don't hesitate to contact a lawyer for advice.*

Insurance Law

Insurance is a special type of contract under which a corporation (the *insurer*) is authorized by law to make an agreement with a person (the *insured*) to *indemnify* or pay the insured, in the event a specified loss occurs as described in the contract.

The insured pays the insurer an agreed amount of money (the *premium*) either in lump sum or in a series of payments over time, and the agreement is evidenced by a written contract (the *policy*). The policy is very important because its terms control the coverage and payment in the event of a loss. Always read the fine print and remember — the insurance agent represents the company, not you.

Insurance companies and the rates they may charge are controlled by state law, and all states have an official "insurance commissioner" or similar official who oversees the operations of these companies. Complaints about insurance companies and agents can be addressed to this official. Among the major problems concerning state regulators are companies that are, or may become, undercapitalized, thus unable to pay claims when they come due.

How a State Insurance Commissioner Can Help

A few years ago, complaints against a respected national life in-surance company began piling up at the offices of insurance com-missioners in several states, including Florida, home to many retir-ees. The grievances came from individuals and organizations who, based on agents' misrepresentations, thought they had purchased retirement income plans. The plans, however, turned out to be straight life insurance coverage — quite a difference! After investi-gation by several state insurance commissioners and the threat of court action, the company was forced to refund millions of dollars to injured customers. Needless to say, the company fired the agents who had misled their clients.

If you have an insurance-related complaint, contact your state insurance commissioner in your state capital.

Insurance can be purchased to guard against almost any loss imaginable, providing the purchaser is willing to pay the pre-mium. The most familiar policies are issued to cover separate risks, such as loss of life, health and medical problems, home owner's liability and auto collision and personal injury.

Life insurance can be an excellent means of estate planning, since the proceeds are paid directly to the named beneficiaries at the death of the insured, are not taxable to them and are not tied up in the probate of the estate, which can often take ex-tended periods of time.

2. Consumer Law

Perhaps the first time the U.S. Congress addressed the issue of "consumer rights" was when it made mail fraud a federal crime in the 1870s. For most of our history, the rule in sales transactions was "let the buyer beware," perhaps a confirmation of Nietzsche's observation that "merchant and pirate were for a long period one and the same person."

The last 30 years has witnessed a blizzard of federal and state laws supposedly designed to protect consumers against dishon-est, fraudulent, deceptive, unsafe and unhealthy products and practices on the part of the business sector. For example, in 1975 Congress passed the Magnuson-Moss Act (also called the "Warranty Act"), setting minimum uniform national standards for disclosure of product warranties and responsibility. The Act covers sales of $15 or more involving personal property purchased for use by families, individuals or households.

Pursuant to the Act, the Federal Trade Commission promulgated rules defining unfair and deceptive trade practices and began taking action against accused businesses. FTC rules require manufacturers to disclose to buyers product testing results, the length of time for product warranties and the remedial procedures available if a product proves to be unsatisfactory. The Act gave consumers the right to sue in state court to enforce these rights.

Product Warranties

When a person purchases personal property, goods or services from a seller in exchange for payment, a contract results in which the seller usually, but not always, gives a *warranty* that basically guarantees the product is not defective. Generally, the law imposes this *implied warranty of performance*, even if no specific statement is made by the seller.

If the product does not perform as claimed, or is defective, this warranty requires the seller to take responsibility for any resulting damages, or to take corrective action. When the seller makes a specific guarantee of a product or service, it is called an *express warranty*.

Under the Uniform Commercial Code (UCC), a body of law governing business transactions, any sale of merchandise of $500 or more in value carries with it a *warranty of merchantability*, meaning the product must be acceptable for the purpose for which it is sold. When a seller knows the buyer is making the purchase for a stated purpose, a *warranty of fitness* for a particular use is imposed on the seller. Any of these warranties can be avoided by the seller by a clear statement made to the buyer that the product has no warranties, or is sold "as is."

Comment: Many businesses, especially those selling electronics and appliances, make a lot of money selling extended warranties at the time of an original purchase. This, in effect, is insurance that if something goes wrong, the product will be replaced or repaired. If you want to pay for this longer warranty, read and understand what you are getting before spending additional money for the warranty. This may not make sense for low priced items but could pay off when dealing with higher ticket items, like a car or digital TV.

What about customer satisfaction? If you are not satisfied with a product, you are still obligated to pay for it unless you specifically reserved the right of personal approval when you bought it. Otherwise, a product only requires the approval that a reasonable person would give under the circumstances, regardless of your personal opinion.

> **Comment:** *You don't have to take your lawyer with you when you go to the appliance store to buy a digital HD television set, but you should always ask the salesperson to give you a copy of the written warranty on the product you are considering. Read the warranty and ask questions before you buy or sign a sales contract. If you encounter trouble getting a product warranty honored, consider small claims court (see Chapter 13), and if that seems unacceptable, a lawyer may be needed.*

Product Liability

Government statistics show that every year many thousands of people lose their lives or are injured in accidents involving the use of consumer products of all kinds.

Until the beginning of the 20th Century, a consumer who suffered injury as a result of a product he or she purchased had few available legal remedies. The applicable rule was *caveat emptor*, meaning "Let the buyer beware." Thus it was the buyer's responsibility to determine the safety of a product. That concept was acceptable at a time when products were fairly simple in construction and design, and the average person had some basic knowledge of what he or she was buying.

But the rule also meant that the middleman sales dealership insulated the manufacturer from liability. Therefore, if a farmer was injured or killed by a defective thrashing machine, his or her family could sue only the dealer.

This all changed in America in 1916 when a brilliant New York Court of Appeals judge named Benjamin Cardozo (later a justice of the United States Supreme Court), wrote the decision in *McPherson* v. *Buick Motor Car Company*, a legal theory quickly adopted by other American state courts. It suggested an idea whose time had come.

Mr. McPherson was injured when the wooden spokes of a wheel on a Buick touring car in which he was a passenger collapsed, throwing him to the pavement. Judge Cardozo reasoned that, regardless of any direct privity between McPherson (who was not the car owner) and Buick, a manufacturer owes a general duty to any person who may use the product to make it carefully, safely, and without any inherent defects. This is known as the *strict liability theory*.

Today, a person injured by a consumer product can sue the manufacturer, even if the injured party was not a direct purchaser from the maker, and even if the party is only an ultimate user, not actually the buyer of the product. In most states, you can sue even if you were not using the product yourself, but are an injured innocent bystander.

Under the *stream of commerce theory* courts now apply, an injured party can sue a product manufacturer, the distributor, a wholesaler and the retail sales outlet.

There are three general types of product defects that produce liability for injury: 1) defects in the way the product was made ("manufacturing defects"); 2) defects in the design of the product; and 3) a failure to inform the buyer of dangerous aspects of the product, or to give complete instructions on its assembly or operation. In some instances, the product may not be defective, but injury may result because of reliance on advertising or other warranties.

There are a number of valid defenses that may limit a manufacturer's product liability. For example, an injured party must have been using the product as instructed.

Comment: *Product liability law is a tricky area, involving not only legal refinements, but difficult scientific and physical evidence matters. If you are injured, be sure to keep and preserve the product which caused the injury, and see a good lawyer as soon as possible.*

Mail Order Contracts

The one rule to remember when making complaints about a mail order purchase is to always put it in writing. The written record you create will serve as a basis for future negotiations and adjustments related to your problem. Unless the seller states otherwise, 30 days is a reasonable time for delivery of a product by mail. Beyond that date, the seller must notify you of the delay and give you the option of canceling. If you cancel, do it in writing. Your money should be refunded within seven business days.

If you receive unordered merchandise in the mail, you are under no obligation to return it. If merchandise comes in the mail in a mutilated package, you should refuse it and write to the seller immediately informing them of the fact.

If you open a package and find your purchase is smashed to bits, return it with a written statement of what you wish to be done (i.e., cancel, replace or refund). It might also be a good idea to take a picture of the package and the contents the way they arrived in case you need to prove that the box arrived damaged.

If the product is not what you ordered, is different than described, or was replaced by a substitute item, you have the right to return it and get a refund. If you think mail fraud is involved, contact your local U.S. post office.

Consumer Credit

A *conditional sales contract* allows a consumer to finance the purchase of a product. Also known as a *retail installment sales contract*, this arrangement allows the buyer to make a nominal down payment, then regular payments for a specified period of time, until the debt is paid in full.

While the buyer receives immediate possession of the goods, the seller retains a *security interest* in them. The Truth in Lending Act requires the contract to describe the product and any warranties, the amount being financed, the rate of interest charged on the financing (usually rather high for this type of purchase), the total cost including interest and other charges and the time and terms allowed for payment.

The contract also gives the seller the right to repossess the property if the buyer fails to make payments. If the buyer has defaulted on his or her payment, and the property is not returned, the seller has the right to be paid the unpaid balance and to be reimbursed for all collection fees and reasonable attorney's fees. The buyer's obligation under such a contract is called a *secured debt*, the property being the security.

Credit Cards

A credit card is simply evidence of a contract between a bank or commercial business and the cardholder. Credit cards allow consumers to borrow money for a period of time to pay for purchases of goods and services. The issuer of the card must inform the cardholder of the terms of the card's use, the interest rate (usually limited by state law) and procedures for correcting erroneous billing. If a card is lost or stolen, most banks will not hold the cardholder responsible of any new charges if he or she informs the issuer of the card as soon as the charges are discovered by the cardholder.

Most banks imposed a maximum amount (typically $500) that can be withdrawn from an automated teller machine (ATM) within a 24-hour period. If the ATM bank card is lost or stolen, most banks will refund the loss if the bank is informed within a reasonable time.

Under the Fair Credit Billing Act, if an erroneous charge is placed on your credit card account, you must inform the card issuer in writing within 60 days of the billing error. The card company has 90 days to either make a correction or inform you in writing why it believes the charge is accurate. If you are unable to convince the company the charge is a mistake, you must pay the amount or your personal credit may be damaged.

The Act also allows a person who charges consumer goods on a credit card to refuse to pay for an item which is defective. The buyer must make a good faith effort to have the seller replace it, but once the seller fails or refuses, the charge need not be paid. The credit card company should, however, be informed in writing about what has happened.

In 2008, the U.S. Federal Reserve Board announced new rules for banks that issue credit cards. The rules were said to remove unfair credit card practices. In 2009, the U.S. Congress passed into law the "Credit Card Accountability, Responsibility and Disclosure (CARD) Act of 2009." Both the new Federal Reserve rules and the CARD Act became effective in 2010.

The provisions of the CARD Act prevented card issuers from raising interest rates retroactively on existing credit card balances. In response, card issuers did one of two things; many card issuers simply raised interest rates before the new law took effect. In addition, card issuers switched many of their fixed-rate credit cards over to variable cards. This allowed them to take advantage of a loophole in the law, which continues to allow interest rate changes on cards with variable interest rates.

Experts say you can expect card issuers to continue to tighten terms and the credit card business becoming increasingly to be perilous to navigate. It's important for cardholders to be proactive and take measures to protect themselves. Read those printed notices that sometimes accompany credit card bills or appear on card payment websites.

Interest rates are controlled by state laws, most of which impose maximum limits sellers and lenders can charge on various types of loans and purchases. The highest rates allowed are usually for unpaid balances on credit cards and installment sales contracts. Charging more for interest than the law allows is called usury, and is subject to various penalties, including refunds of all interest paid.

The federal Truth in Lending Act of 1968 covers all credit transactions, including advertisements, billing, installment sales of four or more payments and leasing by any business which extends credit as part of their billing system. The Act requires full disclosure of finance charges, annual percentage rates of interest and total costs attributable to financing to the buyer before the purchase. Civil damages can be obtained against anyone proven to be in violation of the Act.

The Equal Credit Opportunity Act of 1975 prohibits discrimination and refusal of credit based on race, color, religion, national origin, sex, marital status or because the credit applicant receives public assistance payments such as welfare or Social Security payments.

Credit Records

The Fair Credit Reporting Act requires any business that refuses credit to an applicant to inform that person of the name and address of the credit bureau that supplied the information on which the refusal was based. In turn, the person who is refused credit has a right to receive an explanation of the refusal from the credit bureau, although a fee may be charged to provide this information.

Federal law now requires that the credit reporting agencies, Equifax, Experian and TransUnion, upon request by the individual, supply a copy of an individual's credit record at least once each year. This can be done by contacting the credit agencies online.

Advertisements

Advertisements, in whatever form they appear, are nothing more than a business informing the public of available merchandise at stated prices. State consumer laws make it illegal for a retail business to engage in the practice commonly known as "bait and switch," by which a company misleads consumers by advertising products at one price and then telling the customer who arrives at the store the price is higher, or that an inferior product is available for the advertised price. A store must also have a reasonable supply of an advertised product on hand, unless it states in the ad that supplies are limited.

A customer who believes he or she has been subjected to fraudulent or deceptive advertising should contact the consumer affairs division of the state attorney general's office.

Debt Collection

At some time or another, almost everyone who buys on credit falls behind on a scheduled payment. A friendly phone call from the creditor is usually sufficient to bring the account up-to-date. If a call is not enough, it may soon be followed by a demand letter from the creditor, and then a warning of legal action by the creditor's attorney. If payment is still not made, the account may be "turned over" to a credit collection agency. This means the agency buys the account from the creditor for a discounted amount of the total owed, hoping to make a profit by collecting the total amount.

If the debt owed is under an installment sales contract, the agreement usually contains an acceleration clause, allowing the creditor to demand the entire unpaid amount if the debtor falls behind in payments, even though the contract still has time left.

A creditor's rights for debt collection depend on the terms of the original debtor-creditor contract. If the agreement allows repossession by a seller who has retained a security interest in the goods, once the debtor is notified of his default, the creditor can use "self- help," meaning the creditor can take the goods back.

Often, a debtor does wish to return the goods, although he or she remains liable for the balance owed if the seller cannot resell the goods for the amount that is owed, which he is obligated to try to do. If the debtor refuses to surrender the goods, the creditor must go to court to seek a remedy.

The technical name of the legal action for a secured creditor seeking return of property from a debtor is replevin, under which the court will issue an order to return the goods. The order will be carried out with assistance from the local sheriff.

If the debt is unsecured, the creditor will sue for money owed and will have to prove the contract to the court. If the creditor wins, he receives a judgment from the court, allowing him to execute on the property. The usual means of execution in such a case is *garnishment*, in which a third party, such as the debtor's employer or bank, is ordered to pay to the creditor the amount of the judgment debt out of funds belonging to the debtor.

In addition, a judgment creditor can take possession of and sell any property belonging to the debtor, a process known as *attachment*, or in some states, a *levy*. Most states have laws allowing certain defined *exemptions* of a debtor's property from attachment, including clothing, household furnishings, tools and other equipment up to a certain maximum value. If a debtor appears to have no property that a creditor can attach, the debtor may be required to appear in court for an examination under oath to answer the creditor's questions.

The Soldiers and Sailors Civil Relief Act allows active duty military personnel to have any civil actions pending against them (including debt collection) postponed if it can be demonstrated military service makes it impossible to defend against the civil suit. The Act also halts repossession rights of a creditor. With many U.S. military personnel stationed abroad in recent years there have been media exposés charging that this law was being ignored, with real and personal property taken without notice to indebted military persons.

Under the federal Fair Debt Collection Practices Act, the tactics and activities of consumer debt collection agencies are severely limited. The Act does not apply to collection efforts by the original creditor — only those of an agency to which

Chapter 9

the debt has been assigned or sold. The Act forbids collection agencies to use threats or abusive language, to publish names of debtors or to make false statements or repeated phone calls to the debtor, especially after 9:00 p.m. or before 8:00 a.m. The Act also allows a debtor to state in writing that he or she does not intend to pay the debt and is requesting that collection efforts end. (The collection agency is then bound by this request.)

Such agencies have no right to your financial statement, but they ask for them as a means of finding out where your money is stashed. Collection agencies almost always go after wages and bank accounts, not personal property. Pensions, Social Security income and 75% of take-home pay are exempt from collection agency attachment.

If you owe back taxes to the Internal Revenue Service (IRS), a tax lien can be placed on any property you own, or may later acquire. This means the property cannot be sold or transferred until the lien is fully paid.

More immediate is an IRS levy, which is an attachment of personal property, wages, or bank accounts, requiring no court order. The only exemptions from an IRS levy are as follows: up to $1,650 worth of clothes, personal effects, and furniture; up to $1,100 worth of tools used in business; and payments for disability, unemployment benefits, child support or welfare.

That Dreaded Word: Bankruptcy

The word *bankruptcy* comes from a combination of the Italian words *banca* (meaning "bank") and *rotta* (meaning "broken"), this taken from the Latin, *rupta*, the feminine form of the verb, *rumpere*, "to break." That says it all.

Bankruptcy is a drastic step that tarnishes an individual's credit rating for up to 10 years. Anyone from whom credit is requested has the right to ask whether you have previously filed bankruptcy, and to act accordingly.

Bankruptcy law is almost entirely federal in nature, consuming many volumes of Title 11 of the United States Code. The basic theory of law is that a person in financial trouble (a *debtor*) should be able to reorder his or her economic affairs and have a right to a "fresh start." The losers in this process are the people to whom debts are owed (the *creditors*).

These laws are administered by federal bankruptcy judges who are part of the U.S. district court system. It is with the clerk of the U.S. bankruptcy court that *bankruptcy petitions* (as the filing forms are known) must be filed. Both the federal government and the states, by constitutional or statutory provisions, have adopted exemptions which protect certain property of a debtor from a judgment creditor.

The fees listed below are statutory filing fees, payable to the bankruptcy court. These figures do not include attorney fees, which vary depending upon location, the complexity of your case and a variety of other factors.

- Chapter 7 Filing Fee: $335 (Discharge of most unsecured debts)

- Chapter 13 Filing Fee: $310 (Structured partial repayment plan for debtors who want to keep assets like homes)

- Conversion Fee: $15 (to change a Chapter 13 case into a Chapter 7 case)

- Amendment Fee: $30 per amendment (if you have to make changes to certain documents after initial filing)

Major Law Reforms

The number of 2014 bankruptcy filings, 910,090 cases, dropped a significant 12% from 2013, reflecting reforms imposed by an amended U.S. bankruptcy law in hopes of curtailing fraud and abuse in the system. The Bankruptcy Abuse Prevention and Consumer Protection Act (BAPCPA) took effect in 2005.

The 2005 law applied a "means test" to determine whether a person qualifies for Chapter 7 bankruptcy, which erases debts, or Chapter 13, which establishes a payment system. The goal was to force more people to repay what they could.

Other changes included mandatory credit counseling prior to filing for bankruptcy, requiring pay stubs and tax returns to verify income, and extending the period between when a person can again file for bankruptcy. Critics of the legislation contend that it was a boon to the consumer credit industry and that it did not address the root causes of bankruptcy. The most common reasons behind bankruptcy filings are health care costs, divorce and periods of unemployment.

A previous 1994 revision of the bankruptcy statutes by Congress significantly increased penalties for bankruptcy fraud — such as transfer or concealment of assets now punishable with a fine of up to $5,000 and five years in prison for each instance.

The Homestead Exemption

One of the most significant safeguards a debtor has is the *homestead exemption*, allowed under the laws of all but a few states. Varying greatly in liberality and application, the first of these laws was enacted in Texas in 1839, but all have as their objective preserving a place in which a debtor and his or her family can continue to live, regardless of their economic difficulties.

Under federal bankruptcy law, the state homestead exemption law applicable to the person filing bankruptcy in that state used to be honored. But the 2005 bankruptcy law revision overruled state exemption amounts and limits the state exemption for a homestead to $125,000 if the property was acquired within the previous 1,215 days (3.3 years).

The exemption applies only to real estate owned and actually occupied as a primary residence (usually a single-family home) by a debtor who is the head of a household and his or her family. In many states, a primary residence includes condominiums, co-op apartments, and even mobile homes. Some states now make the exemption available to single individuals as well.

In order to be protected by this exemption, it is necessary to claim it under state law, usually by executing a written declaration which in some states must be recorded in the official land records. In most states, the exemption can be claimed even after a judgment creditor has executed a levy against the property.

Several states do not exempt the home property from debts acquired before the homestead was purchased. The value of the exemption varies according to state law, which sets a stated maximum figure (usually in the range of $1,000 to $20,000) or expresses the exemption in land area terms. New Jersey allows none, Utah very little; but states such as Texas and Florida are well-known for their liberality on this point.

Texas allows an exemption of 200 rural acres plus a home, without regard to value. In cities, it allows land and improvements acquired for $10,000 or less without regard to appreciated value. Written into the Florida constitution is a similar exemption, protecting 160 acres in rural areas, or one-half acre in urban areas, plus the residence located thereon, regardless of actual worth.

Because of the value of Florida real estate, the state has become a Mecca for wealthy persons facing financial problems that move there, invest most of their remaining capital in multi-million dollar horse farms or waterfront residences then file personal bankruptcy, secure in the protection of their new "homestead." Repeated attempts to tighten the homestead law have met a dead end in the state legislature.

In states where the homestead exemption is less generous, nothing prevents the forced sale of a home to pay a judgment creditor, although the homeowner is allowed to retain the dollar amount of the exemption, before the balance goes toward satisfaction of the debt owed to the creditor.

There are several common forms of bankruptcy, each designated by the "chapter" number in Title 11 of the United States Code governing that particular form. Bear in mind, whatever form of bankruptcy is filed, from the moment of filing the law requires all creditors to cease all efforts to collect any debts owed by the filing debtor. This is known as an automatic stay, and failure to observe this debt moratorium can bring down the wrath of the court on the violator.

Types of Bankruptcy

Only the court or a trustee can lift the stay, and this is commonly done for lenders who have pending mortgage foreclosure actions or liens on automobiles temporarily suspended by a bankruptcy filing. This means the lender can get the home or auto back, but the balance of the debt is erased.

Chapter 7: Three quarters of all bankruptcies filed are "Chapter 7" filings. In a Chapter 7 bankruptcy, the debtor surrenders control of all of his or her assets to a trustee appointed by the court. The trustee, a harried lawyer who probably has several hundred bankruptcy cases going at any one time, determines what property is exempt. A Chapter 7 bankruptcy may only be filed once every six years.

Chapter 9

Though it doesn't sound like much, federal law allows a number of important exemptions of property not included in the bankruptcy which a debtor can retain, and creditors cannot reach.

Following are the exemptions under the current law in addition to the homestead exemption:

- The debtor's aggregate interest, not to exceed $18,450 in value, in real property or personal property that the debtor or a dependent of the debtor uses as a residence, in a cooperative that owns property that the debtor or a dependent of the debtor uses as a residence, or in a burial plot for the debtor or a dependent of the debtor.

- The debtor's interest, not to exceed $2,950 in value, in one motor vehicle.

- The debtor's interest, not to exceed $425 in value in any particular item or $9,850 in aggregate value, in household furnishings, household goods, wearing apparel, appliances, books, animals, crops, or musical instruments, that are held primarily for the personal, family or household use of the debtor or a dependent of the debtor.

- The debtor's aggregate interest, not to exceed $1,225 in value, in jewelry held primarily for the personal, family or household use of the debtor or a dependent of the debtor.

- The debtor's aggregate interest in any property, not to exceed $975 in value, plus up to $9,250 of any unused amount of the exemption provided under paragraph (1) of this subsection.

- The debtor's aggregate interest, not to exceed $1,850 in value, in any implements, professional books or tools of the trade of the debtor or the trade of a dependent of the debtor.

- Any un-matured life insurance contract owned by the debtor, other than a credit life insurance contract.

- The debtor's aggregate interest, not to exceed in value $9,850 less any amount of property of the estate transferred in the manner specified in section 542(d) of this title, in any accrued dividend or interest under, or loan value of, any un-matured life insurance contract owned by the debtor under which the insured is the debtor or an individual of whom the debtor is a dependent.

- Professionally prescribed health aids for the debtor or a dependent of the debtor.

A debtor may decide to honor an existing installment contract, lease, or other obligation by reaffirmation, a statement in the filing that the debtor will continue to pay these debts as they come due in the future. Usually the creditor must agree.

After all exemptions are claimed, and all other assets accounted for, the trustee will sell any assets that are not exempt, applying the proceeds on a pro rata basis to remaining debts. All other debts are discharged. Because all creditors are listed in the Chapter 7 filing, each is sent official notice the debts are no longer owed to them.

Under the law, certain types of obligations are considered *non-dischargeable debts*. For example, bankruptcy cannot discharge a debtor of *federal taxes* (unless they are owed for a period more than three years before the date the bankruptcy is filed), *child support* or *alimony* or repayment of most direct or guaranteed *federal student education loans*. Any credit card purchases made within 20 days of filing bankruptcy, and loans or installment sales contracted for within 40 days of filing, are also non-dischargeable.

Non-Dischargeable Debts

If a creditor believes a debtor incurred a debt by fraud, knowing he or she could not pay, or if there is evidence the debtor fraudulently transferred property to third parties prior to filing bankruptcy to avoid payment of debts, the creditor can file an *adverse proceeding*, a hearing at which the court will determine if fraud has occurred. If it has, the court can exempt these debts from discharge, and the creditor may continue to seek payment.

In addition, a debtor who is proven to have committed such acts can be tried and convicted of criminal bankruptcy fraud and sent to federal prison.

Comment: *Chapter 7 bankruptcy is the simplest form of bankruptcy filing. It is done on a multi-page form available at any stationery or office supply store or on the Internet. The* *forms are standard throughout the nation and contain short explanations of what information must be filled in on each page: 1) a list of all assets, real estate, personal property, bank accounts, etc.; 2) a list of all debts and persons or businesses to whom debts, loans, mortgages, etc. are owed. If you don't list the debt and the creditor's name, the debt will not be discharged); 3) a list of all exempt property claimed; and 4) a mailing label list with creditors' names and addresses. If you have very few assets and an accurate list of your debts, you should be able to fill out the forms and file them without the assistance of a lawyer. Be sure to keep several copies of the filing, which must be done in duplicate. When you file, it is done under penalty of perjury.*

The 2005 revision law (BAPCPA) made extensive major changes to Chapter 7 procedure. The major change occurred provided for dismissal (or conversion) of a Chapter 7 case upon a finding of "abuse" by an individual debtor (or married couple) with "primarily consumer debt." The old law provided for dismissal of a Chapter 7 case only upon a finding of "substantial abuse."

The 2005 law defines "abuse" in two ways. "Abuse" can be found when there is an un-rebutted "presumption of abuse" arising under a newly created "means test." The second way to find "abuse" is through general grounds, including bad faith, determined under a totality of the circumstances.

Discharge Ability

BAPCPA also provided more protections to creditors because it expanded the exceptions to discharge. The presumption of fraud in the use of credit cards was expanded. The amount that the debtor must charge for "luxury goods" to invoke the presumption is reduced from $1,225 to $500. The amount of cash advances that would give rise to a presumption of fraud has also been reduced, from $1,225 to $750. The time period was increased from 60 days to 90 days. Thus, if a debtor purchases any single item for more than $500 within 90 days of filing, the presumption that the debt was incurred fraudulently and therefore non-dischargeable in the bankruptcy arises. Prior to BAPCPA, the presumption would not have arisen unless the purchase was for more than $1,225 and was made within 60 days of filing.

The debtor must propose a formal repayment plan demonstrating exactly how monthly payments will meet obligations, even though the payments may be at a reduced rate. The plan is administered by a court-appointed trustee. Secured creditors must be paid 100% of the value of their interest, but unsecured creditors get no more than they would under a Chapter 7 plan.

The Chapter 13 plan does force the debtor to pay unsecured creditors all of his disposable income (any income left over after necessities are purchased). If the debtor cannot keep up payments under the Chapter 13 plan, as often happens, he or she can convert to a Chapter 7, relinquish his or her nonexempt assets and clear his or her debts. Although the same general principles apply, a Chapter 11 bankruptcy is used for business debt reorganization by corporations or partnerships, and a Chapter 12 is used for family farms.

Comment: If you have kept good records, you can probably file Chapter 13 without a lawyer. However, keep in mind that the trustee controls the repayment plan, and you must cooperate with him or her, or the bankruptcy will be dismissed by the court, leaving you open to attach by creditors. Chapter 11 and 12 filings are more complex and normally require help from a lawyer, an accountant, or both.

Chapter 9

CHAPTER 10:
CRIMINAL LAW AND PROCEDURE

Robert Green Ingersoll (1833-1899), American political leader and orator once said, "Laws spring from the instinct for self-preservation."

In no area of jurisprudence is this truer than in criminal law. Criminal law is the cement that holds society together, a statutory definition reflecting the popular consensus of what is acceptable personal behavior. In the largest sense, a crime is a wrongful act or omission injurious to the public welfare, not just harmful to the individual who may be its immediate victim.

Almost all criminal law is state law, created by statute in the 50 states, drawing on legal principles dating back to English common law and even before. The only crimes under the federal government's jurisdiction are those relating to constitutional powers. These include postal service matters, U.S. currency counterfeiting or crimes that occur on federally controlled areas (such as federal prisons, national parks or military installations). There are also interstate federal crimes, such as racketeering, kidnapping and airplane hijacking.

Having stated that most criminal law is state law, it is worth noting an alarming trend that has developed over the past 30 years.

The U.S. Congress, as part of the so-called "war on drugs," repeatedly has enacted laws federalizing certain acts that previously were crimes only under state law, such as possession of certain amounts of marijuana and other drugs. This means a person accused of these crimes can now be prosecuted either by federal or state authorities.

This "federalizing" of crime has now spread to non-drug offenses as well, such as car-jacking, white-collar financial crimes and even environmental offenses. Constitutional scholars and criminal law experts strongly oppose this trend, but the reasons behind the federal "get tough on crime" policies are far more political than legal in nature. Elected politicians want to show that they are "tough on crime" — so they vote to make more and more actions federal crimes.

As an illustration of the federal-state dichotomy, when an anti-abortion demonstrator shot and killed an abortion clinic doctor and another person in Pensacola, Florida, the accused killer, Paul Hill, was convicted of murder by the State of Florida and executed; but he was first tried separately and convicted by the U.S. government for the interstate crimes of gun law violations and interference with access to such clinics the only federal crimes involved.

Criminal law is divided into: 1) *statutory law*, precisely defining the elements which in combination constitute a specific crime; and 2) *criminal procedure*, the extensive body of law and rules governing investigations and arrests by the police, prosecution by the state, and trial, conviction, and sentencing by the judiciary.

1. Statutory Crimes

Common law divides crimes into inherently evil acts (*malum in se*), such as murder or rape, or intrinsically neutral acts the state decides to prohibit (*malum prohibitum*), like fishing without a license. More serious crimes with greater punishment (usually a year or more in prison) are called *felonies*; less serious crimes with less punishment are called *misdemeanors*. More serious than both is the unique crime of treason, the rare attempt to overthrow the federal or a state government by force or violence.

There are two essential elements that must be present in order for a person to commit a crime: 1) the intention to commit the act (*mens rea*) and 2) the act itself (*actus rea*). For example, while murder (the intentional killing of one person by another) is a crime, an accidental killing or killing in self-defense is usually not a crime. Similarly, the mere intent to commit a crime is not in itself a criminal offense, without some overt act.

Certain actions that go beyond mere thought but are not in themselves major crimes are known to the law as "preliminary crimes." The crime of *solicitation* is requesting another person to commit a crime or to assist you in committing a crime.

Conspiracy is an agreement between two or more persons to commit a crime — but it becomes a crime only when at least one party performs an "overt act" furthering the conspiracy, such as buying a gun to be used in a robbery. *Criminal attempt* occurs when a person intends to commit a crime and takes the first step. For example, if an armed man grabs a woman's purse, then lets it go and runs away, it is considered attempted robbery.

A person can be guilty of a related crime, even though his or her role is secondary to that of another person who commits a crime. Anyone who participates in a crime — such as the driver of the "getaway" car in a bank robbery — is an accomplice to that crime. A person who assists another to commit a crime, either by prior planning or later concealing or helping a criminal to escape, is an accessory. In some states, the crime of aiding and abetting is a distinct offense, meaning a person assisting another to commit a crime is also responsible for that crime.

Crimes Against the Person

Crimes against the person include: *assault* (a perceived or threatened attempted harmful touching of another person) and *battery* (the deliberate harmful or offensive touching of another person's body without his or her consent); *false imprisonment* (confining a person's movement against his or her will without justification); *kidnapping* (secretly confining or moving a person from one place to another against his or her will); *mayhem* (intentionally causing the bodily disfigurement of another person); *rape* (sexual intercourse with a person against their will); and *statutory rape* (consensual sexual intercourse with a person under a certain age determined by state law).

There are circumstances under which a person is presumed by the law to have the right to use limited physical force (*corporal punishment*) against another, such as when a parent or school teacher disciplines a child. But if excessive force is used, especially if injury results, it may amount to assault and battery.

Many states no longer permit corporal punishment in public schools, and almost all states have *child abuse laws* requiring reports to the police or child welfare agencies by medical or other personnel who have reason to believe a child has been beaten.

Many states have adopted "Megan's Law" named after a young girl in New Jersey who was molested and killed by a convicted sex offender out on parole. The law requires the state to create an Internet web page to provide timely information to the public on registered sex offenders who reside, attend school or are employed within the state.

Taking a Human Life

Homicide is the killing of one human by another, and it is not necessarily a crime, unless the killing meets the definition of murder or manslaughter. Killing in self-defense, a soldier's killing in battle and an official execution at a state prison are all acts of homicide, but they are not considered crimes.

Murder is the illegal killing of one human being by another "with malice aforethought." That phrase, so familiar from "Law and Order" and other television crime shows and movies, has multiple meanings. *Malice aforethought* includes: 1) intentional killing without legal justification, 2) death resulting when intending serious bodily harm, 3) killing in the course of committing a felony, 4) death resulting from a high-risk action taken with disregard of the consequences, and the 5) killing of a police officer while resisting arrest.

Murder and its punishment are also classified by degree — first and second. *First-degree murder* includes willful and premeditated death ("in cold blood"), killings committed during the commission of certain felonies, and death by poison, explosives, or ambush. *Second-degree murder* includes "spur of the moment" unpremeditated intentional killings ("hot blood"), death resulting when the intention was to do serious bodily harm, and death resulting from "high-risk" activities.

Manslaughter is the illegal killing of one person by another, but without malice aforethought. *Voluntary manslaughter* is intentional but with mitigating circumstances, such as an enraged husband or wife killing a spouse's lover upon discovering them engaging in sexual intercourse. *Involuntary manslaughter* is an unintentional killing, as in the course of criminally negligent conduct, like driving an auto while under the influence of drugs or alcohol.

Crimes Against Property

Crimes against property include: *larceny*, the unlawful taking and carrying away of another person's personal property with the intent to permanently deprive the owner of the property;

embezzlement, the wrongful taking of another's property that has been entrusted to the person taking it; *forgery*, making or altering a legally significant writing, like signing another's name to a check; *burglary*, the unlawful breaking and entering into the dwelling of another with the intent to commit a felony (any felony, not just stealing money); *robbery*, using or threatening immediate force to take money or property from a person; and *extortion*, forcing another person to pay money or do some act under threat of physical harm, or revelation of some harmful fact concerning reputation.

Other crimes involve possession of, or actions against, specific property, like *receiving stolen property*, knowing it to be stolen; arson, the deliberate and intentional burning of a structure; or possession of a *controlled dangerous substance* (i.e. illegal drugs).

There are a host of other crimes, including: *perjury*, lying under oath; *loitering*, hanging around in a public place without purpose; *prostitution*, engaging in sexual activity for money; *bigamy*, marrying a second person when already wed; *incest*, sexual relations with a close blood relative; *adultery*, a married person having sexual relations with a person other than his or her spouse; and d*isturbing the peace*, making a public ruckus.

Defenses Against Criminal Charges

A person charged with a crime has the option of pleading guilty or not guilty. A third alternative is a plea of *nolo contendere*, meaning the accused does not admit the truth of the criminal charge, but submits himself or herself to the jurisdiction of the court for whatever determination the judge may make. If an accused individual chooses to plead "not guilty," there are certain established factual patterns recognized by the law that may negate the criminal charge alleged by the government prosecutors.

A general defense is that the accused did not commit the crime, or the defense may admit the accused did certain acts, but *mitigating circumstances* prevent the conduct from constituting a crime (as in *self-defense*).

As a general rule in American courts, pleading "ignorance of the law" is not a defense. A criminal charge may be excused if a mistake is made regarding a material fact or if the accused was in reasonable fear of immediate great bodily harm or death.

Chapter 10

"Voluntary intoxication" is usually no defense, but it may diminish the seriousness of the criminal charge when intention must be proven.

An *alibi* is, in theory, the perfect defense — some disinterested and creditable person testifies that the accused was at a different place away from the scene of the crime at the time it was committed.

Self-defense is a valid defense to certain criminal charges. Under the law, a person is entitled to use reasonable force to protect himself, or another person, when he or they actually are in immediate danger of harm from another person. This can include "deadly force" in appropriate situations. Many states require the threatened person attempt to retreat, before resorting to using force. And generally, you cannot use deadly force to protect property. You also cannot kill an intruder in your home simply because he is there; he must first pose an immediate threat to you or your family.

From a technical viewpoint, many crimes have a *statute of limitations* that set a period of years beyond which a person cannot be charged with that crime. If the time has expired, this is a good defense.

One valid defense which is well-known, but rarely successful, is a plea of *insanity*. This defense is accepted by a judge or jury in less than one percent of the cases in which it is used.

"Insanity" as used here is a legal term, not a clinical psychiatric description of a mental condition recognized in medical circles. State laws use one of two legal tests to determine insanity.

The first is the M'Naughten Rule (from a case of the same name), which is the oldest legal test. This rule holds that a person who, because of an impaired mental condition, is unable to understand the nature of his or her actions, or who understands his or her actions but lacks the mental capacity to distinguish right from wrong, is not held criminally responsible.

The second states that a person is not criminally responsible if, because of a mental disease or defect, he or she lacks *substantial capacity* to appreciate the criminality of the conduct or to conform his or her conduct to the requirements of the law.

Some states also allow a *diminished capacity* mental defense, which does not excuse criminal conduct, but may lessen the charges or sentence imposed if the accused's mental capacity was partial impaired.

In recent years, juries have begun to acquit criminal defendants based on variations of a novel theory (not authorized in law) that might be called the "victim defense" or the "abuse defense." Thus, the Menendez brothers got a California hung jury after claiming they shot their parents to death because they were the victims of child abuse. (In 1994 the brothers were re-tried, convicted and sentence to life without parole.) And in 1993 Lorena Bobbit was acquitted in Virginia after she sliced off half of her husband's penis while he was sleeping, claiming she was temporarily insane as a result of his abuse and beatings.

In other cases, defendants have claimed their criminal conduct was excusable because it was prompted by television violence, pornography or lyrics of rock music. One woman was acquitted of drunk driving charges after she claimed her condition resulted from her suffering "premenstrual syndrome." None of these defenses have any standing in U.S. law. But juries have a mind of their own and criminal defense lawyers are making the most of it.

Police entrapment is a valid defense to some crimes, such as solicitation for prostitution or selling drugs, when it can be shown that the accused would not have committed the offense except for the police enticement to do so.

Children under the *age of reason*, which the law sets as seven years old, are not considered legally capable of committing a criminal act. Between the ages of 7 and 14, children are presumed not to have capacity to commit a crime, but if it can be shown that the child is sufficiently mature to understand the criminality of the act, he or she can be tried for the crime. Many states allow the option of trying a minor as an adult, depending on how serious the nature and facts of the crime may be.

All states have some form of *juvenile court system* in which minors accused of a crime are tried. In these cases, the major emphasis is on rehabilitation rather than punishment alone.

Chapter 10

A Word About Criminal Defense Lawyers

The unprecedented national attention directed to the O.J. Simpson murder case in this age of television at least provided one unexpected benefit — the education, albeit superficial, of Americans about courts, constitutional rights, criminal law and defense lawyers.

A respected attorney and constitutional expert, Floyd Abrams of New York, suggested in a *New York Times* article that the Simpson case underscored a fact lawyers and judges know all too well — that winning, not necessarily finding the truth, is a defense lawyer's highest priority in a criminal trial.

It is worth considering how our adversarial criminal defense system stands logic on its head. Most people, confronted with a problem, gather all relevant information and reason toward an answer. A defense lawyer, however, is bound to start with an answer — the client's answer — and produce evidence to support that answer. Subject only to the constraints of criminal laws and the rules of legal ethics, a defense lawyer is required to do whatever can be done to defend and vindicate the client's position.

On the other hand, as the U.S. Supreme Court said in a case 60 years ago, the government's interest "in a criminal prosecution is not that it shall win a case, but that justice shall be done." Certainly, that does not always happen.

Whether the system as it now exists needs reform also has many answers. But keep in mind, our Constitution and laws allow — even demand — that possible criminal defenses be raised and exploited.

---

2. Criminal Procedure

The Bill of Rights is the original charter of the basic rules governing criminal procedure still in effect today. These guarantees were meant to protect Americans from being jailed without charges, from being tried without juries and from having their personal liberty, homes and property taken by government agents without just cause.

At the center of the *criminal justice system* is a dual mandate contained in the 5th and 14th Amendments. These Amendments guarantee that no person "shall be deprived of life, liberty, or property, without due process of law."

Due process means that at every step of the government's administration of criminal justice — police investigations, arrest, trial, sentencing, imprisonment, and parole — an accused or convicted citizen's rights must be fully respected and protected.

These rights include, among others: the right to be informed fully of all charges; not to be forced to incriminate one's self; to have the aid of an attorney; to be free from coercion; to confront one's accusers; to be free from unlawful searches; to be able to defend oneself; and to have a fair and impartial trial and jury.

> **Comment:** *If you are charged with a crime, you need the help and advice of an experienced criminal defense attorney. If you are a suspect in a crime, never give the police any information other than your name, address and phone number, unless your attorney approves. If you are the subject of a "custodial investigation" — meaning you are being detained by police and do not have the ability to leave (whether or not you have been charged with any crime) — you have an absolute right to remain silent and to have an attorney present, or to have one provided by the government if you cannot afford one yourself.*

The 4th Amendment guarantees citizens shall not be subjected to unreasonable searches and seizures by government police agents.

Investigation Before Arrest

Evidence produced by an unreasonable search cannot be used against you in a state or federal court under the *exclusionary rule*. If the police attempt to use such evidence, a judge must first rule on the question of the legality of the search before the evidence is admitted or excluded. The issue of admissibility is raised by a *motion to suppress* evidence, made by the attorney for the accused. That decision will turn on what the court finds to be "unreasonable."

Under the exclusionary rule, not only can illegally obtained evidence be excluded at trial, but any other evidence which flowed from that original illegally obtained evidence can also be excluded, even if legally obtained later. This is known as the *fruit of the poisoned tree* exclusionary doctrine.

The entire rule is often criticized as a technical loophole by which criminals go free. But in fact, statistical analysis shows success in less than one half of one percent of the cases in which it is tried. On the other hand, the rule acts as a mild restraint on police who know they can be challenged in court for an illegal search.

Chapter 10

What about *polygraph* or so-called "lie detector" tests? Because of their inherent scientific unreliability, very few courts will admit these test results as evidence. And for a time, some state courts would not admit DNA (deoxyribonucleic acid) tests as conclusive scientific evidence against an accused in a criminal trial, but most now do. Indeed DNA evidenced has been used to prove innocence and obtain the release of numerous persons convicted of crimes they did not commit.

Whether on land or water, a police officer does not have an unrestricted right to stop you, your motor vehicle, or boat, unless he or she has *reasonable grounds* or suspicion to believe that you have committed, you are now committing, or you are about to commit a crime.

The courts have carved out two very large exceptions to this general rule. The first exception is the random use of police road blocks (called "sobriety check points") at which all drivers are stopped and briefly examined to see if they are driving while under the influence of drugs or alcohol. A second exception allows police officers to board public transport (a bus, train, or plane) and request passengers to submit to searches of their person and/or baggage. However, a person does not have to permit these searches.

When you are stopped, an officer cannot search your person (bodily search, or "pat down") without your consent unless there is reason to believe you are carrying a concealed weapon. If an officer searches you for a weapon without good reason and finds an illegal drug on you instead, the search is illegal, and the drug evidence cannot be used.

You never have to consent to a police search of your person, your vehicle, or your home — and you never should as a matter of principle, whether any incriminating evidence might be found or not. And no one else can consent on your behalf.

Even if a parent consents to a search of a minor child's personal possessions, such as a locked closet or trunk, resulting evidence of illegal conduct cannot be used against the minor.

If you do consent to a police search, you can revoke that consent any time after it begins. Keep in mind that once you've given consent to a search, anything found can be and probably will be used against you. If the police wish to search your home, office, or other property, the 4th Amendment requires them to go before a magistrate or judge and show *probable cause* supporting the issuance of a *search warrant*. Courts have defined "probable cause" as being reasonable grounds for the belief in the existence of certain alleged facts — a basis for belief slightly more firm than mere suspicion.

A search warrant authorizes nothing more than a police inspection of the premises in order to determine if any evidence of a crime exists, usually in advance of a criminal charge being lodged against a suspect. The warrant must describe the exact place to be searched and the objects sought. No other objects can be taken during the search, although they often are.

If the police appear at your door with a search warrant, you have a right to read it for accuracy and to see what they are looking for. If you find the warrant to be inaccurate (wrong name, wrong person, wrong address), you should immediately and clearly state these mistakes as the basis for your objections to the search. At that point, the police are likely to continue the search anyway, and the issue of a defective warrant will have to be determined later in court. Especially in the so-called "war on drugs" police searches of the wrong address have been common.

Police do have an immediate right to search if they are legally in a place and see a criminal object in plain view. The police also have a right to search your motor vehicle or motor home (even without a warrant) if they have probable cause to believe the vehicle contains contraband (weapons, drugs) or evidence of a crime, as when someone makes a street drug buy and drives away in a motor vehicle.

For example, if a person is stopped for a traffic violation and found to be intoxicated, police have a right to search the car. The arrested individual may also be strip searched at the police station by an officer of his or her own sex, if there is probable cause to believe he or she may be concealing something illegal.

Police can wiretap your phone and "bug" your house electronically, and later use the evidence so obtained if they get a search warrant authorizing this activity. They can also listen and record a phone conversation if one party authorizes it.

Privacy is Dead in America

The discussion in these pages about the 4th Amendment and its supposed protections against "unreasonable searches and seizures" is now largely an academic exercise. Americans now know that we are all under constant 24-hour surveillance by the government and various police agencies.

In 2013, Edward Snowden, a former contractor to the Central Intelligence Agency (CIA) released to the media a trove of classified information he had taken from the secret files of the National Security Agency (NSA). It was one of the most momentous leaks of top secret U.S. government information in history. Tens of thousands of documents provided evidence of years of illegal mass invasions of privacy by the NSA, both in the United States and worldwide.

The NSA claims their authority for this massive secret spying on Americans is the 2001 PATRIOT Act adopted by the U.S. Congress less than six weeks after the 9/11, 2001 terror attacks. Panicked to "do something" Congress adopted a 362-page law, sight unseen, with few members having the courage to oppose one of the worst attacks on American liberties ever enacted into law.

In spite of massive public opposition to the law, it was extended in 2006 and 2011 at the urging of both Presidents George Bush and Barack Obama, respectively, with majority support from both political parties in the Congress.

All the talk about search warrants and probable cause is now largely meaningless. A prudent American should assume that everything he or she does or says, every phone call, email or letter, is open to police inspection. Flying over an urban area, police planes can pinpoint the location of a single number amid a million or more cell phones.

Using the USA PATRIOT Act, the NSA demands and receives access to all the billions of records from telephone service providers such as Verizon, AT&T or Sprint on an "ongoing, daily basis." That includes our calls and emails. The NSA has built a $1.5 billion data storage center at Bluffdale, Utah, five times the size of the U.S. Capitol building, to process our data.

The Federal Bureau of Investigation (FBI), also thanks to the PATRIOT Act, makes liberal use of National Security Letters (NSLs), an "administrative subpoena" that allows its agents to demand information considered "relevant" to their investigations. The FBI can learn anything it wants from anyone with whom you do business, your bank, your cell company, even your own company, and you won't know anything about it, because it is a federal crime to tell you that they've been asked.

Back in the old days, the word most often associated with government surveillance was "wiretap." It evokes images of J. Edgar Hoover's fedora-hatted G-men with old-fashioned headphones listening in on a bad guy's phone calls from a van across the street.

These days, the word "wiretap" rarely makes an appearance. That's because the government itself no longer needs to do anything technical to obtain information about you. Instead, it orders the companies that provide us with communications, banking, commercial or other services to hand over whatever they have stored on their Internet servers. All it takes is one of those FBI National Security Letters, or some other secret, extra-judicial demand, and it's all surrendered to the government.

Everything we say and do, online and off line, is recorded and stored somewhere. The GPS chip in your smartphone allows for close tracking of your location, right down to the aisle you're walking down in Target. Your credit cards and loyalty cards are tracking your specific purchases. The NSA have hacked SIM card encryption keys and can gain access to your life as conducted over your smartphone without the permission, or even the knowledge, of telecommunications companies or other government agencies. NSA has placed embedded "back doors" inside computer chips in thousands of new computers allowing them constant access to each PC.

The initial media and public reaction after whistleblower Edward Snowden's bombshell revelations about domestic NSA spying was widespread shock and consternation at the extent of the U.S. government's invasion of its citizens' privacy. Two years later, however, very little has changed — except that the public debate and media coverage has been brought largely under control and dominated by the established powers-that-be.

One can guess what James Madison, the author of the Bill of Rights would say, were he to see what has happened to freedom in America.

If You Are Arrested

If police have reasonable grounds or suspicion to believe that you have committed, you are now committing, or you are about to commit a crime, they can arrest you. In addition, police are authorized to use such force as is reasonably necessary if a person resists arrest.

If you are a criminal suspect or if you are arrested, you cannot be questioned by police until you are given a verbal *Miranda warning* describing your right to remain silent, that your statements can and will be used against you, that you have a right to an attorney and that one will be provided if you cannot afford to hire one, and that you can exercise these rights at any future time during the questioning. You must also respond when asked if you understand these rights.

Although the U.S. Supreme Court has held that failure to identify oneself when asked by police is a basis for arrest, never volunteer any statements; always use your constitutional right against self-incrimination and remain silent. Don't even protest your innocence. Give your name, address, and phone number. That's all. Never say anything else until you talk to your lawyer.

An accused individual is protected by a rule known as the *attorney-client privilege*, meaning a lawyer cannot and must not ever reveal the communications made to him or her by a client. The only exception is if the client is asking advice or making statements to his or her lawyer about an intention to commit a crime in the future, in which case an attorney may be obligated to inform the police.

If you are arrested, you will be taken to the police station to be *booked* — photographed, fingerprinted, and allowed one phone call that should go to your lawyer or the person most likely to help you immediately. If your alleged crime is minor, you may be able to *post bail* immediately, meaning payment of a bond to assure you will show up on the appointed court date. For example, a first offense DUI charge may require a bail bond of $500. Once paid, you are released, assuming you have sobered up. If you don't have the money, a bail bondsman will post it for you in return for payment of 10% of the total bond and may ask for collateral as well. If the crime is serious, bail will most likely be very high, and the bail bondsman may require the deed to your house as "collateral" for the bail.

Posting Bond After an Arrest

1. Use your one phone call to contact the person most likely to give you immediate help.

2. Ask him or her to arrange to post bond if one is required. Depending on the seriousness of the crime, a police magistrate or a judge may have to set the bond at a hearing at which you and your attorney have a right to be present. In most jails, bail hearings are held at least once a day, excluding weekends, so you might have to wait for 24 hours or more, depending on when you are arrested.

3. When the court sets the bail bond amount, it must be paid either by you, your friend, or a bail bondsman. Many courts now accept credit card payment, but they check to see if your credit is good for the amount involved. The

bondsman's fee will be a nonrefundable 10 percent of the total bond.

4. When the bond is paid to the court clerk, you will be set free with instructions to appear on a stated date for further court proceedings. Within two to four days after the arrest, the arraignment takes place, during which you appear before a magistrate or judge, who informs you of the charges against you and your right to counsel. He or she will also ask whether you wish to enter a plea of guilty or not guilty. A third plea possibility is nolo contendere, meaning you do not admit the truth of the charges, but you submit yourself to the court's jurisdiction for whatever sentence the judge may think appropriate. No plea should ever be entered until you consult with an attorney.

A person is formally charged with a crime by: 1) the filing of a criminal complaint signed by the arresting officer or a "complaining witness," usually a person who has been injured by the crime; 2) an indictment issued by a grand jury after an investigation; or 3) a judge or magistrate at a preliminary hearing to determine "probable cause."

Going to Trial

In order for a court to try an accused, it must have *jurisdiction*, over both the person (who must be in custody or on bail) and over the crime alleged. For example, a state or federal court sitting in Utah cannot try a person for a crime alleged to have been committed in Nevada, because the court has no legal right or power to do so.

If an accused is arrested in one state for a crime committed in another state, unless he or she agrees to being returned for trial, Article Four of the Constitution requires there be a formal extradition proceeding — a hearing on whether the accused should be surrendered to the requesting state. Only the governor of a state has the power to extradite an accused person.

The 6th Amendment guarantees you the right to a "public and speedy trial." If charges are more serious, an accused individual may waive the speedy trial requirement in order to have more time to prepare a defense. It is not unusual for a criminal trial to begin as long as a year after the charges are first made.

Chapter 10

A defendant has a right to a *jury* composed of his or her "peers," which the Supreme Court has held to mean a reasonable cross section of the community. This does not mean a jury must contain members of the accused's race, religion, sex or national origin — but it certainly does mean no person can be excused solely for those factors. If that happens, a new trial may be ordered on appeal. Jurors must be unbiased, have formed no prior opinion of the case, and be able to state their ability to decide impartially after hearing the facts.

Under our justice system, a person must be proven guilty *beyond a reasonable doubt* in a criminal trial, the highest standard of evidence. The accused has a 5th Amendment right against self-incrimination allowing him not to testify, and the prosecution cannot comment on this lack of testimony. At all stages of the criminal justice process, the accused is *presumed innocent until proven guilty*.

Prior to trial, the prosecution or defense may propose a *plea bargain* in order to avoid the time and cost involved in a trial The state may offer to drop some of the charges or reduce the seriousness of the charges, or recommend a reduced sentence to the judge in return for the defendant's agreement to plead guilty or to give evidence against another defendant.

Depending on the evidence supporting the charges against the accused, a *plea bargain* may be the best way to minimize punishment. In most areas of the nation, the great majority of criminal cases are resolved with plea bargains. In a recent calendar year in New York City alone, less than 4,000 felony cases went to trial out of a total of over 21,000 felony arrests. Many people object to this practice because it invariably means the accused receives a far shorter sentence, or no jail time at all but it also keeps the court system from collapsing under the sheer volume of potential criminal trials.

Unless the charge against you is a *petty offense* (punishable by six months or less in jail), you have a "right to trial by jury," also guaranteed by the 6th Amendment. Most states require 12 jurors who must unanimously agree on a verdict, but some states allow six or eight jurors for less serious offenses.

The 6th Amendment also guarantees the right to confront and cross-examine accusers, to subpoena witnesses, and to compel them to testify. The state must provide the defendant with all evidence so the accused can prepare for trial. If a defendant feels the exclusionary rule should apply to any evidence, he or she has the right to request the judge to rule on these objections before or during the trial. If a case has been prejudiced by pre-trial publicity, the defendant can seek a *change of venue* (a relocation of the trial to another area) or ask for a *gag order* preventing anyone associated with the case from making statements to the news media.

The procedural order of a criminal trial is much like that in a civil trial:

- Jury selection;
- Opening summary statements by the prosecution and the defense;
- Presentation of the prosecution's case, evidence, witnesses' statements, and cross-examination by the defense;
- Presentation of the defense's case, cross-examination by the state;
- Closing summary statements by the defense and then the state, which always has the right to go last;
- Instructions by the judge to the jury on the applicable law;
- Jury deliberations and verdict, or no verdict and deadlock.

A person who has been tried and acquitted of a crime cannot be tried again for the same crime, because the 5th Amendment to the U.S. Constitution prohibits placing a person in *double jeopardy*. You can be tried again, however, if at the first trial the jury was deadlocked ("hung"), or if the judge declared a *mistrial*, or if you are granted a new trial on appeal after conviction.

If the federal government has a "unique interest" in a case that resulted in a state acquittal, the federal government may also try the defendant for such crimes as counterfeiting, violations of alcohol prohibition laws and criminal violence in labor disputes.

Chapter 10

If a defendant is found guilty, there may be grounds available to challenge the verdict by motions made to the trial court, or for review on appeal to a higher court. The usual grounds for overturning a criminal conviction and granting a new trial are: the prosecution's withholding of *exculpatory evidence* from the defense; a judge's *mistake in jury instructions*; admitting excludable evidence which should have been suppressed; admission of prejudicial evidence (such as a prior criminal record irrelevant to the current charges); or discovery of new evidence after trial.

Sentencing, Prison & Parole

Traditionally in America, judges have had a large measure of discretion when imposing punishment on those convicted of or who plead guilty to crimes. This latitude in administering justice was based on the idea a judge has the advantage of presiding over an entire trial, thus gaining a first-hand impression of every factual and legal aspect of the case — and of the defendant.

While statutory law sets a maximum punishment for each crime, in the past judicial discretion allowed imprisonment for less than the maximum time, for no time at all, for fines, restitution where appropriate or placing the defendant on probation — or a combination of all of these.

Nevertheless, in the last 20 years, state and federal legislators have passed numerous laws requiring *minimum sentences*, especially for drug-related crimes, thus removing the judge's discretion in sentencing. Another tactic has been the "three strike" laws providing for permanent incarceration when a person is convicted a third time for an additional crime, regardless of how inconsequential the third crime may be.

In addition, parole allows a prisoner, once incarcerated, to earn early release for good behavior, and executive clemency allows the President or a state governor to commute a criminal sentence for similar or for humanitarian reasons. The powers of parole boards and state governors in such matters are almost never questioned by the courts.

Under the 8th Amendment, criminal punishment cannot be *cruel and unusual*, defined by the Supreme Court as any punishment that "shocks the conscience" and "offends fundamental notions of human dignity" — life in prison for stealing a loaf of bread, for example, as in Victor Hugo's *Les Miserables*.

The Sentencing Reform Act of 1984 established a commission which recommended mandatory sentence guidelines of varying severity for over 3,500 different federal crimes. These guidelines took effect in 1987, essentially tying the hands of federal judges when imposing sentences for these crimes.

Not to be outdone by the states, Congress passed laws imposing statutory mandatory sentences for specific crimes — including the "three strikes you're out" provision, specifying life sentences for repeat drug offenders.

Lastly, a word about the writ of *habeas corpus*, a traditional all-purpose criminal procedural remedy restricted by recent court rulings. A prisoner files this ancient common law writ with the court of appropriate jurisdiction seeking release based not on guilt or innocence, but on an allegation he or she is incarcerated in violation of some specific constitutional right — denial of the right to legal counsel, a coerced confession, treatment constituting cruel and unusual punishment. If a court grants relief in response to the writ, it usually does not allow release from custody, but it may order the state to provide the constitutional remedy the prisoner seeks.

If All Else Fails

Chapter 11:
Dealing with the Government

In many situations, dealing with the government may be unavoidable. If it becomes necessary to correspond with a government agency, make sure to document thoroughly your actions and communication. Keep copies of all records, make a note of the names and titles of all federal employees with whom you talk by phone and keep a journal of these contacts and what is said. Always mail all correspondence "return receipt requested" so that you have proof of where it went. At some point, you may need this information which could prove decisive in getting what you want.

Suing the Government

The legal doctrine known as *sovereign immunity* has been carried over from English monarchs into American law. This legal principle provides for government immunity from citizen litigation. For many years, Congress selectively granted permission to individual citizens, one case at a time, allowing each to file suit in the U.S. Court of Claims, but only after the Senate and House passed, and the President signed, a *private law*. (A "private law" is a law limited in its scope and effect to one or a few individuals, as compared to a "*public law*" that applies generally to all citizens.)

This meant that before a person injured by a government agent could even go to court, he or she had to convince the U.S. Congress of the merits of the case. State governments were held by courts to have similar protection from citizen litigation.

The obvious inequity of such a situation eventually produced calls for reform. In 1928, New York became one of the first states to enact a law creating a special claims court to handle such suits. At first, Congress waived immunity only for motor vehicle injury suits, but the volume of claims bills being introduced continued to expand as society became industrialized and accident prone.

In 1948, Congress passed the Federal Tort Claims Act (FTCA), waiving government immunity from suits involving any negligent or intentional act by a federal employee or agent causing personal injury and property damage. The provisions of the FTCA must be followed carefully in order to preserve an injured citizen's legal rights. In most cases, the Act requires the filing of an administrative complaint against the specific federal agency whose employee is accused of wrongdoing, before a suit can be filed in federal court.

Does a citizen with a claim have a chance of success against a federal agency? The answer is yes.

For example, in one 10-year period the U.S. Department of Veterans Affairs paid out more than a quarter of a billion dollars in damages under the FTCA because of thousands of medical malpractice claims against VA health care providers. In one year alone, 801 new VA claims were filed, and $41 million was paid for past claims, lawsuits and settlements. While the VA is perhaps more susceptible to personal injury claims because they run the largest hospital and clinic system in the nation, other federal agencies also can be forced to pay.

Watch out for the statute of limitations on filing claims against the government. It's stricter than the statute of limitations for filing a private suit. The general FTCA deadline is one year from the date of the injury, or from when the injury becomes reasonably apparent. State laws impose similar filing deadlines for claims against the state.

The FTCA does not grant a wholesale right to sue the government. For example, active-duty military and naval personnel (and their dependents) are prevented from suing for claims arising out of their military service. While there is a reasonable excuse not to allow servicemen to sue for injuries from military combat (they are eligible for veterans benefits), the FTCA does not permit a claim by a serviceman or his family injured by medical malpractice occurring in an Army or Navy hospital.

Comment: *If you are considering filing a personal injury or property damage claim against a federal agency, contact the legal department of that agency and obtain a standard federal* *tort claim form. The instructions that come with the form should enable you to file any small claims amount yourself. Evidence of damages, such as medical or hospital bills, or repair costs for damaged personal property should be attached to the form, which requires a total dollar amount claimed. If the claim requires special scientific or medical evidence to support it, you may wish to consult a personal injury lawyer for assistance. Government lawyers are required by law to respond to all such claims within six months. If the claim is denied, you can file suit in U.S. district court. Most federal agencies try to settle tort claims without going to court.*

A person who is qualified under the law may be eligible for retirement, disability or death benefits under the federal Social Security system. The system is financed in part by payroll taxes paid by 9 out of 10 American workers, including those who are self-employed. A person's qualification for benefits depends on credit obtained during his or her work life measured in the total number of "quarters" of each year during which he or she worked and paid payroll taxes. Depending on the calendar year in which a person reaches the age of 62, the required number of quarters differs. For example, a person turning 62 in 2008 or later must have worked 40 nonconsecutive "quarters" (or 10 years) under Social Security taxes in order to qualify for retirement benefits.

Social Security, Retirement & Disability Payments

Retirement benefits are based on a person's highest years of earnings; the more a person earned, the more he or she qualifies to receive. A person married more than one year may qualify for auxiliary benefits based on a retired spouse's Social Security eligibility. When a person eligible for Social Security payments dies, his or her spouse and minor children may be eligible for survivors' benefits.

**

> **Comment:** *You can contact the Social Security Administration (SSA) yourself (without a lawyer's help), or you can appoint a family member or friend to represent you. This initial contact is necessary to start the administrative process. Social Security retirement benefits usually begin automatically once you reach the age 65.*

The Social Security Administration is one of the largest bureaucracies in the federal government based on total number of employees and dollars paid out to eligible citizens. Like most government agencies, it suffers from inefficiency. If you have trouble getting satisfactory help from SSA, you should notify your U.S. Senator or Congressman. The SSA jumps when the office of a member of Congress contacts them, so you should see fast results.

Medicare & Medicaid

Medicare is a national program of hospital and medical insurance run by the federal government for people 65 and older and those disabled for a certain period of time, regardless of age. If you are eligible for Social Security retirement or disability payments, you may also be eligible for Medicare, but you may have to apply for enrollment.

Medicaid is a joint state and federal medical welfare program, eligibility for which depends on total income and assets, rather than age.

There is also a federal program known as Supplemental Security Income (SSI), eligibility for which is based on age, serious disability, and poverty level income and assets. It is administered through the Social Security system.

The Patient Protection and Affordable Care Act (PPACA), or Affordable Care Act (ACA), became law 2010. Also called "ObamaCare," the goal was to provide health care insurance coverage for all Americans. A Rand Corporation study concluded after five years, that of 43 million people who were uninsured in 2013, 25.8 million Americans still had no insurance in 2015 and 5.9 million had lost coverage.

Unemployment Benefits

If you are not self-employed and are laid off from your job, depending on how long you worked and your income level, you may be eligible for unemployment payments. These benefits are administered by the state government and not available to workers who voluntarily quit, unless they can show their employer coerced them into resigning.

The level of unemployment benefits is based on a combination of federal and state law, but you must show proof you are continuing to look for new employment in order to receive payments. If you refuse a job reasonably suited to you based on your age, education and experience, you could lose your benefits. If benefits are refused or withdrawn, there is an appeal procedure for contesting the action.

U.S. Internal Revenue Service

Don't fool around when contacted by the IRS about taxes owed. The best rule is to have your attorney or accountant contact the IRS on your behalf, never make contact yourself. If you receive a notice in the mail, have your lawyer call the phone number on that notice and discuss the situation, (if they are lucky enough to get someone to answer). He or she will try to reach some agreement about what is to be done immediately, and will follow up the phone call with a confirmatory letter restating the understanding of the agreement.

> **Comment:** *Whenever you correspond with the IRS always send letter with "Return Receipt Requested" so that you have proof that you sent the document. If the IRS claims you owe federal taxes, interest and penalties, either convince them they are wrong or make acceptable arrangements for payment. Otherwise, the IRS can place a tax lien on any property you own or may later acquire, such as a home or a car. This means you cannot sell or transfer the property until the lien is fully paid. When the IRS issues an order for a levy (an attachment of your personal property, wages, or bank accounts), no court order is needed, and the person, employer or bank must hand over the levied property or money immediately.*

One last word about the IRS: in recent years the IRS has prosecuted successfully hundreds of cases in which individuals claimed that the tax laws were invalid and/or did not apply to them. This "tax protest" movement is to be avoided, lest you increase your tax bill with added interest and penalties or even be sent to prison.

Chapter 11

Workman's Compensation

When a worker is injured or killed while on the job, federal and state law offers a system which in theory may provide immediate payment to the worker, or to his or her survivors. Over 90 percent of all workers are covered by such laws, although certain classes (including domestic household employees, farm workers, temporary employees, volunteers, and people employed by nonprofit groups) may be exempted in some states.

Workman's compensation laws require employers, in return for a legal guarantee they will not be sued for on-the-job injuries, to either purchase insurance or contribute to a state fund out of which workers are compensated for harm caused during work.

An individual is eligible for compensation provided he or she is an employee of the company involved and not an independent contractor or a temporary worker hired through an agency. Benefits under workman's compensation laws are based on the seriousness of the injury and its permanence. For example, there are well-established tables indicating the value of a lost finger or of suffering emotionally from work-related stress. If you are injured at work, immediately notify your employer and request the forms to file a workman's compensation claim.

You should not need an attorney in this situation. But if your claim is denied or given a ruling less than you think fair, you should hire an attorney who specializes in such claims.

Information & Privacy

The 1966 Freedom of Information Act in theory gives every citizen the right to seek and obtain certain classes of information contained in government agency files, although searching and copying fees may be required. In certain situations (such as an ongoing criminal investigation), the government can withhold information, but they must explain their refusal to divulge.

You must address your formal request for specific information in writing to the federal agency which has such records. (See sample request on next page.) Names and addresses of all federal agencies and their national, regional and local offices are contained in a federal publication called the *Government Organizational Manual*, available in any public library or online.

Generally, it takes many months at some agencies to obtain information because of the massive number of requests and the low priority bureaucrats place on such requests, law or no law. You might want to call your congressman's office if you encounter trouble. According to the Associated Press in 2015, "The systems created to give citizens information about their government are badly broken and getting worse all the time."

Freedom of Information Act Request

Date: ____

Freedom of Information Act Request Representative

(Address in full of government agency)

Re: Freedom of Information Act request

Dear Sir/Madam:

In accordance with the federal Freedom of Information Act, I hereby request a copy of all records containing information on me as may be maintained in your files.

I will pay all reasonable searching and copying fees associated with this request. However, if total cost is expected to exceed $[X] amount, Please advise me in advance of the cost.

Thank you for your cooperation.

Sincerely,

Your signature

Your name printed

Your Social Security number

Your address

Your area code and telephone number

Any previous name(s)

Recent previous address(es)

The Privacy Act of 1974 requires the government to use information about a person only for the purposes authorized by law. If it is used otherwise, a citizen can force correction of information that is erroneous. Federal law does allow multiple uses of information about a citizen, often as a way of uncovering fraud.

For example, in 1989, Congress authorized a computer cross-check of names and income amounts of people receiving poverty-level veterans' benefits and actual income reported to the IRS on individual tax returns. As a result, tens of thousands of people were caught fraudulently receiving veterans payments to which they were not entitled based on their true income. Similar computer cross-checks are done for delinquent student or other federal loans.

Under the terms of the 2001 PATRIOT Act the government has the virtually unlimited power to request and obtain any information it wants about financial matters. Banks and other institutions are forbidden to inform you of such requests. The net effect of this is that personal privacy in America is dead and gone.

Immigration Law

The federal government has, in theory, the power to control the immigration and naturalization of foreigners allowed to become new U.S. citizens. Immigration laws are administered by the U.S. Immigration and Customs Enforcement Service (ICE), an agency within the U.S. Department of Homeland Security, a cabinet level department created by Congress in 2002.

In 1991, Congress adopted a reformed immigration law, authorizing a general amnesty for illegal aliens living in the U.S. for five years or more. In recent years controlling unwanted immigration become a major national political issue, as millions of illegal aliens have entered the United States. So far, no new law has been adopted because the continuing differences over how best to deal with major immigration issues. An estimated 12 million illegal aliens now reside in the United States.

The 1991 reform law created an annual quota of new immigrants of 226,000 persons, with preference granted to relatives of U.S. citizens and permanent resident aliens. An additional 140,000 quota is available to persons with "extraordinary" or "exceptional" talents in science, the arts and commerce, and to those willing to invest $1 million or more in job-producing businesses.

Foreign nationals can be refused entry into the U.S. for many reasons, including insanity, drug addiction, communicable diseases, criminal records, indigence and illiteracy. If a person is admitted as a resident alien, he or she can become a citizen five years after application. Until then, he or she is given a "green card" allowing him or her to obtain employment. (It is a crime for employers to hire aliens who do not have a green card.) Citizenship can also be obtained by marrying a U.S. citizen.

If you, or someone you know wishes to become a U.S. citizen, contact the INS office listed in the government blue pages of the phone directory or online and ask for pamphlets explaining the process. There is also extensive information on the Internet at the ICE web site.

Comment: Applying for assistance from the ICE sometimes means risking deportation, depending on a person's status. Some lawyers may be able to speed up the process and obtain a faster response, but they often charge fees ranging from $5,000 to $15,000, depending on what is required. It would be wise to first check with private organizations and public service law groups who specialize in helping people with immigration problems. They know the law and often offer free advice.

Although the Constitution creates only three branches of government — the legislative, executive, and judicial — there is another major part of government some people call "the fourth branch." This branch is said to include the many federal and state agencies which are "administrative" in nature. These agencies have the power to make and impose rules and regulations having the force of law, within certain broadly defined policy objectives outlined by the laws delegating such authority.

This sort of governmental arrangement unfortunately allows un-elected and unknown government officials and employees a great deal of latitude in implementing policy, while having little or no accountability to the people. It has also given rise to an extensive body of law known as administrative law, which tries to define how much power such agencies have been given, whether they exercise that power properly and fairly, and the degree to which administrative agency actions are able to be reviewed by the courts.

In order for regulations to be adopted legally, the government agency must strictly adhere to the statutory process for proposing rules, publishing them for public comment in the *Federal Register*, (see Chapter 2) and putting into effect such rules. All parties effected by such rules must be given adequate public notice of exactly what is proposed and a chance to offer their views in writing or in person at public hearings.

Administrative Law

Chapter 11

CHAPTER 12:
CIVIL RIGHTS

The United States Constitution confirms each American citizen's natural God-given, fundamental, and inalienable rights. Included among these individual rights enumerated in the first 10 Amendments to the Constitution (known as "the Bill of Rights") are: freedom to practice the religion of choice, freedom of speech and peaceable assembly, freedom of the press, the right to bear arms, the right to due process and equal protection of the laws, the right to be secure in our homes, and the right not to have property taken without payment of just compensation.

In addition, the 13th and 14th Amendments abolished slavery ("involuntary servitude") and guaranteed the right to vote to all citizens, respectively.

Subsequent interpretation of the Constitution by the U.S. Supreme Court and statutory enactments of Congress have established a host of other "civil rights," as they are now called. These include freedom from discrimination based on race, color, religion, sex or national origin in voting, education, employment, public accommodations, transportation and housing.

It should be understood that none of these rights are absolute in and of themselves but may be reasonably restricted by government when there are compelling reasons to do so. A classic example of such a limitation is the observation that freedom of speech does not allow a person to cause panic and injury by falsely yelling "Fire!" in a crowded theater.

Freedom of Religion

The First Amendment establishment clause prohibits the government, not only from establishing a national religion, but also from favoring one religion over another and from hindering a religious practice.

Under the First Amendment, the wall of separation doctrine demands the least possible degree of official association between church and state. Under this legal concept, the government attempts a "benevolent neutrality" toward religion, neither opposing nor promoting it.

Based on Supreme Court decisions, this policy allows laws giving tax-exempt status to religious institutions, and even some limited financial aid for religious schools. But it also prohibits the location of religious displays on public property (such as a Christian nativity scene on a court house lawn), unless it is part of a larger secular display.

Free exercise of religion means government will not dictate how a church should conduct its affairs, unless there is some "compelling interest" to do so. A good example of this is when the polygamy practiced by the Church of Jesus Christ of the Latter Day Saints (the Mormons) was outlawed by federal statute.

The Court has also held parents responsible for the death of a sick child, even though their religious beliefs dictated that no medical assistance ever be used. And the U.S. Air Force can prevent an orthodox Jewish airman from wearing a yarmulke while in uniform because of a rule forbidding the wearing of religious symbols in the military.

The first 10 Amendments to the U.S. Constitution guarantee the basic rights, freedoms and protections of every United States citizen.

The Bill of Rights

AMENDMENT I

Congress shall make no law respecting an establishment of religion, or prohibiting the free exercise thereof; or abridging the freedom of speech, or of the press; or the right of the people peaceably to assemble, and to petition the Government for a redress of grievances.

AMENDMENT II

A well-regulated Militia, being necessary to the security of a free State, the right of the people to keep and bear arms, shall not be infringed.

AMENDMENT III

No soldier shall, in time of peace be quartered in any house, without the consent of the owner, nor in time of war, but in a manner to be prescribed by law.

AMENDMENT IV

The right of the people to be secure in their persons, houses, papers and effects, against unreasonable searches and seizures, shall not be violated, and no Warrants shall issue, but upon probable cause, supported by oath or affirmation, and particularly describing the place to be searched, and the persons or things to be seized.

AMENDMENT V

No person shall be held to answer for a capital, or otherwise infamous crime, unless on a presentment or indictment of a Grand Jury, except in cases arising in the land or naval forces, or in the Militia, when in actual service in time of War or public danger; nor shall any person be subject for the same offence to be twice put in jeopardy of life or limb: nor shall be compelled in any criminal case to be a witness against himself, nor be deprived of life, liberty or property, without due process of law: nor shall private property be taken for public use, without just compensation.

AMENDMENT VI

In all criminal prosecutions, the accused shall enjoy the right to a speedy and public trial, by an impartial jury of the State and district wherein the crime shall have been committed, which district shall have been previously ascertained by law and to be informed of the nature and cause of the accusation: to be confronted with the witnesses against him; to have compulsory process for obtaining witnesses in his favor and to have the Assistance of Counsel for his defense.

AMENDMENT VII

In suits at common law, where the value in controversy shall exceed twenty dollars, the right of trial by jury shall be preserved, and no fact tried by a jury shall be otherwise reexamined in any Court of the United States, than according to the rules of the common law.

AMENDMENT VIII

Excessive bail shall not be required, nor excessive fines imposed, nor cruel and unusual punishments inflicted.

AMENDMENT IX

The enumeration in the Constitution, of certain rights, shall not be construed to deny or disparage others retained by the people.

AMENDMENT X

The powers not delegated to the United States by the Constitution, nor prohibited by it to the States, are reserved to the States respectively, or to the people.

The Supreme Court upheld the right of the Santeria Church to sacrifice live animals and birds as part of its rituals, despite a local ordinance forbidding this practice out of concern for cruelty to animals and health considerations. The Court has also allowed the traditional use of an otherwise illegal hallucinogen drug (peyote) as part of services in the Native American (American Indian) church.

One of the most controversial interpretations of the First Amendment was the Supreme Court's ruling that laws requiring or permitting prayer or Bible reading in public schools are unconstitutional. The Court also ruled that a child cannot be forced to pledge allegiance to the U.S. flag, if doing so would violate his or her religious beliefs.

A state law was passed prohibiting employers from requiring workers to work on their Sabbath. But the Supreme Court struck it down, because in their view, this meant the state was forcing private businesses to conform to one religion's beliefs.

On the other hand, the Court has consistently upheld state and local "blue laws" forbidding certain commercial business or sales on Sundays. The theory behind this is that such laws are grounded not in religion but in state labor policy, allowing workers a day of rest each week.

In 2014, the Court upheld a Catholic order of nuns' objections to the Obamacare requirement that they must pay for health insurance coverage that provides for birth control, payments that directly violate Catholic teachings and beliefs. The Court also held that the arts-and-crafts retailer, Hobby Lobby, could opt out of the Obamacare contraception insurance mandate for religious reasons.

If you are confused by the foregoing discussion of Supreme Court decisions concerning the constitutional meaning of freedom of religion and the separation of church and state doctrine, you are not alone. These cases reflect the continuing difficulty the Court — and all Americans — have had trying to reconcile religion and politics.

Freedom of Speech

The First Amendment guarantee of freedom of speech goes well beyond the right to say what you please, write, hold rallies or even criticize and advocate the overthrow of the American government. This guarantee now extends to actions the Supreme Court defines as symbolic speech including dancing, book burning or even burning the American flag. The First Amendment, however, does not allow such things as slander, libel or solicitation of another person to commit a crime. And if public speech presents a "clear and present danger" of imminent criminal conduct — as when a fiery speaker turns a crowd into an unruly mob bent on violence — the police have the right to take action to stop the speaker.

Although the right to peaceable assembly is also guaranteed by the First Amendment, local governments are allowed to require a permit for certain public meetings, and even to impose a fee for costs of police protection for the gathering and to set time, place, and length of duration restrictions. The organizers of "Woodstock II," for example, needed numerous New York State, local and police permits before the enormous crowds were permitted to wallow in the mud and rock 'n' roll. But legally, government cannot even attempt to control the content, program or other aspects of such a gathering.

The Right to Bear Arms

In 1789, when this phrase was written into the Second Amendment, it referred only to a citizen's right to take up arms to defend the nation as an active member of a citizen militia. In those days, before intercontinental ballistic missiles, a citizen militia was the only means of defense available. Every part time citizen soldier kept his musket at hand. It was these citizen militias that won America's independence from England.

Despite the controversy over a citizen's unfettered right to own hand guns and automatic weapons, the Second Amendment does not grant an unrestricted right to private gun ownership.

Government has the inherent "police power" to regulate private gun ownership, just as it does other weapons, such as knives and explosives. Government also has the power to license guns and gun owners, and to impose reasonable waiting periods and investigations before gun sales are allowed to become final. In 2008, in the case *District of Columbia* v. *Heller*, the U.S. Supreme Court ruled for the first time that the Second Amendment guarantees individual's right to possess firearms, holding that it was unconstitutional for the D.C. government to prohibit the private ownership of guns. In *McDonald* v. *Chicago* (2010), the Court clarified its earlier decisions expressly holding that the Fourteenth Amendment applies the Second Amendment to state and local governments to the same extent that the Second Amendment applies to the federal government.

Despite these decisions, the heated debate between various organizations regarding gun control and gun rights continues.

Other Rights

U.S. citizens have a general right of freedom to travel, both domestically and abroad. Some travel restrictions can be imposed for valid reasons by a court, such as when a person is out on bail awaiting trial, or when child custody has been granted to one parent over another. International travel may also be restricted when a nation is at war or in conflict with the United States. The U.S. State Department constantly issues "travel advisories," warning Americans against going to areas of the world judged to be unsafe.

When travelling internationally, there are numerous restrictions you should consider. It is a crime, for example, to leave or enter the United States with $10,000 or more in cash or negotiable securities on your person, without reporting this to the U.S. Immigration and Customs Enforcement Service (ICE). If you do report such an action, you can expect to be questioned by Customs, the Drug Enforcement Agency, the FBI and all sorts of officials. You must also report purchases made abroad and their estimated value on standard Customs Forms when returning to the U.S., and perhaps pay import duties, depending on the total value.

Lastly, a word about the right to privacy. The word "privacy" is not mentioned in the Constitution, although the 4th Amendment, in the context of forbidding unreasonable searches and seizures, guarantees "the right of the people to be secure in their person, houses, papers and effects…"

In the 1973 Supreme Court decision legalizing abortion, a majority of the justices found an inherent right to privacy as one of the grounds on which to base their holding. In 1986, the Court in *Bowers* v. *Hardwick* upheld by a vote of 5-4, a Georgia state statute making private consensual sexual activity between adults of the same sex a crime, finding no right to privacy in such a bedroom situation. This ruling was subsequently overturned in 2003 in *Lawrence* v. *Texas* that reversed the Georgia case ruling.

It is fair to say the right of privacy is a developing area of the law to watch closely as a judicial barometer of how far "Big

Brother" government will be allowed to go in the regulation of our private lives. As noted previously, the PATRIOT Act has abolished financial privacy when it comes to government snooping into our affairs. The disclosure of sweeping surveillance by NSA has prompted a wave of lawsuits challenging the U.S. government's intelligence gathering programs.

> **Comment:** *If you feel your civil rights have been violated, you may want to contact your local chapter the American Civil Liberties Union (ACLU). This organization specializes in defending constitutional rights — especially if there is a broad question that potentially affects many citizens. You may also want to lodge a complaint with the Civil Rights Division of the U.S. Department of Justice in Washington, D.C. The office of any United States Attorney can be found online under Federal Government, and can give you further information and advice. In certain cases, the nature of the alleged violation will dictate where a complaint should be filed.*

Chapter 12

Chapter 13:
Civil Suits and Small Claims

I n this chapter, we discuss what happens during a civil law-suit and how you could act as your own lawyer in small claims court. These situations revolve around two or more private parties in a dispute, who turn to the court system to assist them with an official determination of their rights and liabilities.

How a Civil Suit Progresses

Before we discuss court procedures, let's review the judicial process of a *civil suit*, which is a legal action relating to private parties seeking remedies for a violation of their rights.

The *statute of limitations* is the time period during which action to remedy a wrong must be initiated, or the right to take action is forever foreclosed. It varies in each state and with the subject matter at issue. For example, in the case of an alleged breach of an oral contract, various state laws range from 2 to 10 years; a written contract, 3 to 15 years; for personal injury torts, 1 to 6 years; for a claim against the federal government, as little as 60 days in some cases, usually up to one year under the Federal Tort Claims Act discussed in Chapter 11. If you do not file your suit within the time the statute requires, you are out of luck.

If you are within the statute of limitations time period, the first step in a civil suit is the filing of a *written complaint*. This document sets forth the cause of action — the factual and legal basis of your claim. For example, the cause of action might explain what a contract said and how it was violated. The complaint also makes a claim of damages and asks the court to award you an amount of money or some other relief, such as ordering the wrongdoer to live up to the contract (specific performance). The parties to a complaint are the *plaintiff* (the one complaining of a wrong) and the *defendant* (the one accused of a wrong).

210 Lawyer-Proof Your Life

If a false complaint is filed, you (and your lawyer) could be sued for the tort of *malicious prosecution*, and the judge can impose *sanctions* (a money fine or other punishment) on your attorney who should have investigated the merits of the case before he or she filed.

A complaint must be filed in the office of the clerk of the court which has *jurisdiction* over the subject matter and parties to the suit. Most civil matters, for example, are filed in *state courts*, civil division, because state law governs this type of private dispute.

Once a complaint is filed, the court clerk issues a *summons* informing an alleged wrongdoer of a suit and its nature. These must be *served*, meaning personally delivered to the defendant. The defendant has a time period set by law (usually 30 days) in which to file an *answer* to the complaint. If he or she does not, the plaintiff may win the case without further proceedings, other than a motion informing the court of the defendant's failure to respond and asking for a summary judgment.

A *summary judgment* states that when read together, the complaint and answer offer enough evidence to decide the case on those pleadings alone. A similar motion which accomplishes the same purpose is a *motion for judgment on the pleadings*. Sometimes a defendant will not file an answer but instead will respond by filing a demurrer or a motion to dismiss, which essentially replies with, "So what?" By doing so, the defendant contends the complaint does not state a cause of action sufficient to allow the suit to go forward.

The court can rule immediately on a *demurrer* and end the case or, more likely, it will allow an *amendment* to the complaint following a hearing. If an amended complaint is allowed, it must be served, and the defendant has another 30 days to answer.

Before a civil trial starts, a period known as *discovery* begins during which both parties use the *rules of civil procedure* to obtain records, documents and information bearing on the subject of the suit. This can include submission of written questions a party must answer called *interrogatories*, or questioning of parties or potential witnesses under oath by the opposing party's attorney outside of court, known as a *deposition*. Depositions are recorded and transcribed into a written record, and may even be videotaped.

If a party resists a request for a deposition, the court may be asked to issue a subpoena to force testimony or a *subpoena duces tecum*, requiring the production of specific records and documents. A person who lies under oath in a deposition (or in later court testimony) can be charged with the *crime of perjury*, which is a felony in most states.

As in the case of the criminal evidence exclusionary rule, motions can be made prior to a civil trial to exclude certain types of evidence which might be *prejudicial*. More than 90% of all civil disputes are settled out of court, often even before the suit is filed. This is because few people want to risk a trial with all its attendant delays, costs, uncertainties and publicity.

If a suit goes to trial, the first order of business is *jury selection*, during which prospective jurors are questioned, usually by a judge, to ensure their competency, impartiality and fairness. Jurors may be excluded for a number of specific reasons (*for cause*) or for no reason at all (called a *peremptory challenge*).

As in a criminal trial, a civil trial opens with summary statements by attorneys for the plaintiff and defendant outlining the complaint and the defense. The plaintiff's lawyer then presents the *case in chief*, calling witnesses who may be cross examined by the defense. This is followed by the defendant's case and witnesses.

At the close of either the plaintiff's case or the defense, motions can be made asking for a *directed verdict* based on the state of the evidence then before the court. In effect, a lawyer who makes this motion says to the judge, "No reasonable person can dispute the facts presented. Based on those facts Your Honor, you, rather than the jury, immediately should rule in favor of paying damages to my client." Unless the evidence is overwhelming one way or the other, the court usually will not grant such a motion.

Throughout a trial, it is important that both parties' lawyers make appropriate motions and object to any procedure or testimony thought to be improper, stating their reason for doing so. This preserves on the record the right to appeal the judge's rulings in each instance.

Rulings governing the admissibility of evidence go to the heart of a fair trial. These rules have grown in number and complexity over centuries of common law and statutory interpretation.

It is the judge's responsibility to apply the large body of procedure and law known as *the rules of evidence*.

Some of the more familiar evidentiary rules include *relevancy* (the evidence must relate to a material issue in the case), *hearsay* (a statement made at trial by a witness, based not on personal knowledge but on what another person said) and *privileged communications* (between husband and wife, lawyer and client, doctor and patient, confessor and penitent).

If a judge wrongly admits evidence that should be excluded, this could be grounds on appeal for a reversal of the trial verdict, the granting of a new trial or, sometimes, a directed verdict for one party or the other. More often, if an appeals court finds evidence wrongly admitted, it will not reverse the decision in the case, but rather will hold the admission to be a "*harmless error*." In civil trials, the standard of proof required is proof by a *preponderance of the evidence*, which is an evidentiary standard meaning "more likely than not" the facts are true as presented.

Once both sides have concluded their presentations, the judge will give *instructions* on the applicable law to the jury, which then retires to consider the law and the evidence and to reach a verdict. The jury or the judge selects a foreman who presides during the secret jury deliberations and later announces the verdict, if there is one. It is possible for a jury to be *deadlocked* or "hung," meaning no verdict was reached.

If the jury finds against the defendant and for the plaintiff, the defense can move for a judgment *non obstante verdicto* — a judgment for the defendant "notwithstanding the verdict" — meaning the jury's verdict is clearly wrong. If this is denied by the judge (as it usually is), the only recourse for the defendant is to appeal to a higher court, which is a separate procedure after trial.

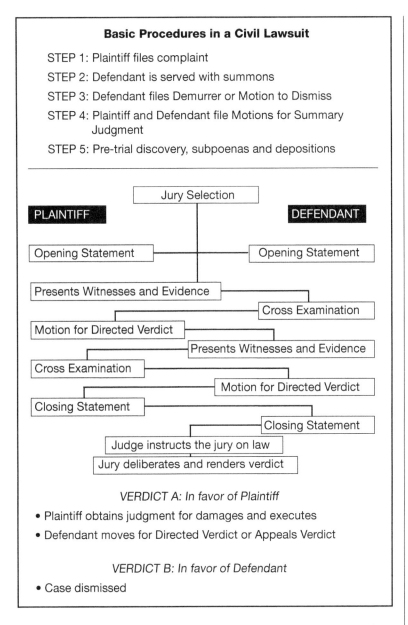

Basic Procedures in a Civil Lawsuit

STEP 1: Plaintiff files complaint

STEP 2: Defendant is served with summons

STEP 3: Defendant files Demurrer or Motion to Dismiss

STEP 4: Plaintiff and Defendant file Motions for Summary Judgment

STEP 5: Pre-trial discovery, subpoenas and depositions

Jury Selection

PLAINTIFF   DEFENDANT

Opening Statement   Opening Statement

Presents Witnesses and Evidence

Cross Examination

Motion for Directed Verdict

Presents Witnesses and Evidence

Cross Examination

Motion for Directed Verdict

Closing Statement

Closing Statement

Judge instructs the jury on law

Jury deliberates and renders verdict

VERDICT A: In favor of Plaintiff

• Plaintiff obtains judgment for damages and executes

• Defendant moves for Directed Verdict or Appeals Verdict

VERDICT B: In favor of Defendant

• Case dismissed

The winning plaintiff will receive a certified copy of the court's judgment containing the terms, such as a money judgment, that are enforceable against the defendant. This makes the plaintiff a judgment creditor with the power to attach bank accounts and property owned by the defendant. In this situation, a winning plaintiff should move quickly to collect, because debtors have been known to conceal assets or even file bankruptcy.

Chapter 13

Small Claims Court

In describing the long and costly process followed in a civil suit and trial, we assumed the issues were so important (meaning the amount of money was so large) that a full-blown legal battle was worth waging.

What if right is on your side and you are fighting mad, but the amount in dispute is a mere $250 or $500. For example, if your car wasn't repaired correctly, and you were forced to take it elsewhere at greater cost, what should you do? If a realistic assessment of your situation supports the conclusion that the facts of your case match the applicable law, why not be your own lawyer and go to court?

Every state and the District of Columbia has established a judicial forum (usually called small claims court) where civil cases involving money claims up to a maximum statutory amount can be filed, litigated and decided — without a lawyer and with simplified procedures.

The maximum dollar amount for cases to qualify for consideration in these courts ranges from $10,000 to $15,000 in Tennessee, to a more common amount of $1,000 to$5,000 in most other states. You can file suit if greater amounts are involved, but these are the maximum recovery amounts allowed for a successful plaintiff.

Often a plaintiff with an amount claimed greater than the maximum will still go to small claims court because of the simplified procedure and speedy decision. Fees for filing suit in these courts often range up to $100 or so.

The first question to ask yourself before filing in small claims court is one any lawyer would ask after examining all the facts: "Do I have a case (cause of action) that will support a reasonable chance of winning?" If not, forget it. To determine a total of potential damages, add up medical expenses, lost wages and damaged personal property. Don't forget to add an amount for pain and suffering. Or, if a breach of contract is involved, figure out what it cost you because of the violation.

Usually small claims court procedure will require you to make a formal written demand for payment to the potential defendant before filing the complaint. You must show proof of this demand when you file the complaint. Of course, you should attempt to settle before suing.

If you decide to file a complaint, be sure you are suing the right parties — especially if the defendant is a corporation, partnership or some other business entity. The office of secretary of state has custody of corporate records, which include the name of the person on whom legal process is to be served. Usually, you can obtain this information by calling the state capital or it may be found online.

Which small claims court you file in depends on the type of cause of action. If you are suing in tort for personal injuries, the complaint should be filed in the county (or judicial district in some states) where the defendant lives or does business, or where the accident occurred.

If you are suing on a contract, you can file the complaint in the judicial district where the defendant lives or does business, where the contract was signed or where it was to be carried out.

Often a contract will stipulate where a suit must be filed and what law applies if more than one state is involved.

Once the complaint is accepted by the clerk of court and your filing fee is paid, a certified copy of the complaint must be personally served on the defendant within a set number of days (usually 15 to 30). Local procedure will govern the service period and the time the defendant has to file a response (again, usually 15 to 30 days).

You can personally serve the papers on the defendant yourself, or you can pay to have it done by a process serving firm. Look under "process servers" in your online search. If you are served with a complaint as a defendant, call the plaintiff and try to settle. If you cannot settle, call the court with any question you may have about how long you have to respond or when a trial date is set. Both facts are usually contained in the service papers, so read them carefully. Most small claims courts do not require a written response you can just show up on the appointed day and orally argue your defense.

But it is much better if you file a written answer the judge can consider along with the complaint before the hearing. The key to your winning the case is good preparation. The first thing to do is frame the issues in the case: Was the defendant's negligence the proximate cause of your injury? Did the defendant breach the contract and, if so, how?

Study the facts, gather supporting evidence and witnesses who agree with your version of the relevant events and analyze the law and its exact application to the facts. Always be sure of exactly what a proposed witness is going to say. Have proof of the total amount of damages claimed — doctor bills, hospital charges less medical insurance reimbursement (if any), repair bills, etc. Remember, unlike a criminal trial where the standard of evidence is "beyond a reasonable doubt," civil trials usually require only a preponderance of the evidence — "more likely than not."

Judges in small claims court often use very informal procedures. If your complaint is clear and supported with attached documentary evidence, the judge may not even ask you to orally present your case or call witnesses. He may turn to the defendant and demand his version, after which you may be allowed to "rebut" these statements. Don't get argumentative beyond bare necessity with the defendant, and never with the judge. Stay cool, analytical and factual — and make it fast. Judges hear scores of these cases each day, and they do not like delay or parties who cause it.

Once you get your judgment, give the defendant a week or so to pay up if he or she doesn't do it on the spot. (The judge will usually demand to know when payment will be made.) Failure to pay should be greeted by you with a written seven-day demand, a statement of your intention to return to court to seek enforcement of the judgment, plus court and other costs. If you are a defendant and pay up, be sure to get a satisfaction of judgment receipt from the plaintiff when you make your payment.

If the defendant does not pay up, you will be forced to find out what assets he or she has and where they are located (the best sources are bank accounts and wages). Banks and employers are legally obligated to pay available funds belonging to a judgment debtor to a judgment creditor, once they have been given a demand and a copy of the judgment accompanied by a writ of execution (another clerk of court form you can obtain easily and fill out).

If the defendant seems to have no assets, you can serve him or her with a "Judgment debtor's statement of assets" form, to which he or she must truthfully respond under pain of perjury. If the defendant has a business, you can get the sheriff's office to send a deputy to take cash out of the business's register on the spot or to take personal property not exempt under local law.

GLOSSARY

Abuse of Process — An actionable tort of using the judicial system for an improper purpose, such as harassment by filing multiple lawsuits without merit.

Acceleration Clause — A clause in an installment sales contract allowing the seller, at his or her option, to demand and receive immediate payment of the entire balance due if a periodic payment is not made by the debtor.

Acceptance — An agreement to the terms of an offer resulting in a valid contract.

Accessory — One who incites or assists another to commit a crime, either by prior planning ("before the fact"), or later concealing or helping a criminal ("after the fact").

Accomplice — One who participates in a crime in any way, whose guilt is the same as the one who actually commits the crime.

Accord and Satisfaction — An agreement settling a claim or lawsuit.

Acquittal — In criminal law, a finding by a judge or jury that an accused person is not guilty.

Administrative Law — See *Law, Administrative*.

Admissibility — The issue of whether proffered facts or other evidence will be presented during a trial, governed by a body of procedural and substantive law known as the "rules of evidence."

Adoption — The legal procedure by which all rights and duties of the natural parents over a child are absolutely terminated, such rights and duties being transferred to the child's adoptive parents.

Adultery — A misdemeanor crime in most states consisting of voluntary sexual intercourse between a married person and a person other than his or her spouse.

Advance Directive — A pre-written document addressed to health care providers expressing the signer's wishes concerning the type and extent of medical treatment to be rendered to that patient when in a terminal or extreme state of medical decline.

Adverse Possession — A method of acquiring title to another's land by open, hostile and continuous use or occupation for an extended period of years.

Adverse Proceeding — A U.S. bankruptcy court hearing on a creditor's claim of fraud or other wrongdoing by a debtor in bankruptcy.

Advertisement — A public informational notice promoting a product or service and legally considered to be an invitation for offers.

Affidavit — A written statement sworn to before a notary attesting to the truth of the facts contained therein.

Agency — A relationship through which one person (*the principal*) gives another person (*the agent*) the right to act in his or her behalf so as legally to bind the principal.

Age of Reason — The age at which the law considers a child to be capable of distinguishing between right and wrong and, therefore, capable of committing a criminal act.

Agreement, Conditional Sales — An installment sales contract in which the seller retains title to the personal property until the buyer pays the purchase price in full.

Agreement, Premarital — A contract between a man and woman prior to marriage, setting forth the division of their property in event of a divorce.

Agreement, Separation — A document governing the obligations and rights of a husband and wife who are separated.

Alibi — A plea by an accused that he or she was elsewhere other than at the scene of a crime at the time it was committed and is, therefore, not guilty.

Alimony — A spousal support allowance paid to one spouse by the other, pending or after a legal separation or divorce.

Animal, Domesticated — Any breed of animal raised to live and breed in a tame condition.

Annotated Code — See *Code*.

Annotated Statutes — See *Statutes*.

Annulment — A judicial declaration that a marriage is and was invalid from its inception due to some basic legal impediment.

Arbitration — The impartial determination of a controversy by a neutral third party empowered by the contestants to decide the issue.

Arraignment — An appearance before a magistrate or judge at which a person accused of a crime is informed of the charges against him or her and is permitted to answer or plead to the charges.

Arrest — Depriving a person (usually one accused of a crime) of his or her liberty by government authority.

Arson — The crime of intentionally burning a structure.

Articles of Incorporation — See *Incorporation, Articles of*

Assault — A deliberate attempted or threatened battery, causing the victim to have fear or apprehension of immediate danger and harm.

Assumption of Mortgage — The transfer of rights and duties under an existing mortgage to a subsequent purchaser of real property, usually requiring the approval of the lender.

Assumption of Risk — A theory of tort law denying an injured person recovery of money damages for his or her injury if that person voluntarily exposes himself to a known danger.

Attachment — The post-judicial civil procedure by which personal property is taken from its owner pursuant to a judgment or other court order.

Attempt — A criminal act by a person intending to commit a crime that falls short of the intended crime itself.

Attorney at Law — A member of the bar authorized to render legal advice and conduct legal proceedings on behalf of others.

Automatic Stay — An absolute prohibition against any further creditor's efforts to collect debts owed taking effect when the debtor files bankruptcy.

Bail — Money or other security paid to a court as a guarantee a defendant released from custody in a criminal proceeding will appear on the appointed date.

Bail Bond — A formal document guaranteeing the appearance of a defendant in a criminal proceeding or, in the alternative, the payment of money to a court.

Bailment — The delivery of property by its owner (the *bailor*) to another person (the *bailee*) for some specific purpose, after the accomplishment of which the property is returned to the owner.

Bankruptcy — A procedure filed in U.S. bankruptcy court whereby a person or other legal entity declares an inability to pay debts and asks that the debts be discharged or restructured to allow payment over an extended period of time.

Battery — A deliberate, offensive, or harmful touching of another person without his or her consent.

Beneficiary — One designated to receive income from a trust estate; also, one named in an insurance policy to receive proceeds or benefits.

Bequest — A gift of money or personal property by will.

Bid — An offer to purchase at a stated price.

Bigamy — The act of marrying without first obtaining a legal divorce from a previous spouse.

Bill of Rights — The original 10 amendments to the U.S. Constitution, adopted by Congress in 1789.

Binder — A brief written agreement to sell real estate at a stated price.

Blackmail — See *Extortion.*

Breach of Contract — The unjustified failure to perform a promise or other contractual obligation.

Brief — A written document prepared by an attorney and addressed to a court, usually a statement in support of a client's position.

Burglary — The unlawful breaking and entering into a structure of another with the intent to commit any felony or misdemeanor larceny.

Cause of Action — The factual and legal basis for a claim in a civil suit.

Change of Venue — Geographic relocation of a criminal trial to a court in another area, usually to avoid the effects of prejudicial pre-trial publicity concerning the case.

Chapter 7 — A form of personal bankruptcy in which a debtor's assets are sold to satisfy existing debts, and remaining unpaid debts are then discharged completely.

Chapter 13 — A form of personal bankruptcy in which a debtor's debts are rescheduled and paid over a period of up to three years under supervision of a trustee.

Chattel — An article of personal property.

Child Custody — The right and duty to care for, control, and provide maintenance of a child awarded to a person (usually a parent) as part of a divorce or separation proceeding.

Child Support — The obligation of a non-custodial parent to contribute economic support for a minor child, usually in periodic money payments.

Citation — An official notice or order to appear in court; also, an identification assigned to an individual legal case or statutory provision giving the specific series of books, the volume, and page number at which such information appears.

Civil Suit — A non-criminal legal action in which one party seeks remedies for personal injury caused by another party or for a violation of contractual or other personal rights.

Civil Union — A legal union of a same-sex couple sanctioned by a civil authority.

Clemency — The power of an executive government official to reduce or commute a criminal sentence or other punishment.

Closing — See *Settlement.*

Code — A printed official government series of statutes or regulations having the force of law. An *annotated code* contains references to all judicial decisions interpreting the statutory provisions of the code.

Codicil — A document supplementing or modifying an existing last will and testament.

Glossary

Collection Agency — A private business that purchases at a discount an existing overdue account from a creditor hoping to profit by collecting the total amount due from the debtor.

Comity — The informal and voluntary recognition by a court of one jurisdiction of the laws and judicial decisions of another court.

Commercial Lease — See *Lease, Commercial.*

Commercial Paper — Any written evidence of valuable ownership or title to personal property capable of being transferred or negotiated with or without endorsement by the holder of the paper.

Common Law — See *Law, Common.*

Community Property — In certain states, property acquired during marriage and jointly owned by both spouses, each with an undivided one half-interest.

Comparative Negligence — See *Negligence, Comparative.*

Compensatory Damages — See *Damages.*

Complaint — A formal document setting forth the alleged facts and cause of action in a civil suit or criminal indictment.

Condemnation — The procedure by which private real property is taken by the government under the powers of eminent domain.

Conditional Sales Agreement — See *Agreement, Conditional Sales.*

Congress, United States — The bicameral legislative body (Senate and House of Representatives) created in Article I of the Constitution.

Consideration — The inducement to a contract or other legal agreement, consisting of an act or forbearance, or the promise thereof, done or given by one party in return for the act or promise of the other party.

Conspiracy — A criminal plan between two or more persons to commit an unlawful act.

Constitution, United States — The basic charter creating the federal government and containing guarantees of citizen rights and protections.

Contempt of Court — Any act that obstructs a court's administration of justice, either committed in the presence of a judge or away from court.

Contract — A binding agreement between two or more parties.

Contract Not to Compete — An agreement in which one party agrees not to compete in business with another party within a geographic area for a specified period of time.

Contract of Sale — An agreement to buy and to sell property (especially real estate) on stated terms.

Contributory Negligence — See *Negligence, Contributory.*

Conversion — The crime of illegal and unauthorized use of another's personal property, usually involving money held in a fiduciary or other custodial capacity.

Cooperative ("Co-op") — A form of joint ownership and management of real property (usually a multi-unit residential building) by a corporation whose shareholders also own the individual units.

Copyright — The exclusive legal right to reproduce, publish, and sell intellectual property, such as musical, literary, or other artistic works.

Corporal Punishment — The use of physical force against a person's body, usually as a disciplinary measure.

Corporation — A business, professional, or other entity recognized in law to act as a single legal "person," although composed of one or more natural persons, endowed by law with various rights and duties.

Corporation, Subchapter "S" — Under federal tax law, a small business corporation that elects to have the undistributed taxable income of the corporation taxed as personal income for the shareholders, thus avoiding payment of corporate income tax.

Corpus — The property owned by a fund, trust, or estate.

Counteroffer — A return offer made by one who has rejected an original offer.

Creditor — One to whom a debtor owes money or other valuable consideration.

Crime — A statutorily prohibited wrongful act or omission that harms a victim and the public welfare.

Criminal Complaint — A formal allegation made to a magistrate or judge by a prosecutor against a named party, which serves as the basis for an arrest.

Criminal Procedure — The body of law and rules governing the process of investigation, arrest, prosecution, trial, conviction, and sentencing of a criminal defendant.

Damages — Money payment recovered in a court action by a person who sustains injury to his or her person, property, or rights through the unlawful or wrongful act of another. *Compensatory damages* reimburse the injured person for actual loss or expenses. *Punitive damages* are added amounts awarded as compensation to punish a defendant for a serious wrong. *Special damages* are provable costs such as lost wages, medical expenses, and hospital bills.

Debtor — One who owes another (a *creditor*) a money amount or other valuable consideration.

Deed — A formal written document signed by an owner conveying title to real estate.

Deed of Trust — A deed signed by a purchaser of real estate used in some states as security for a purchase money loan, wherein the title is transferred to and held by a trustee until the loan is repaid.

Deed, Quitclaim — A deed transferring any interest a grantor may have in real property without guarantees of title, if in fact any interest does exist.

Deed, Warranty — A deed conveying real estate in which the seller guarantees he or she has a marketable title and promises to defend against any title defects that may arise.

Defamation — A false statement by libel or slander which damages a person's reputation.

Defendant — An accused person who is required to make a formal answer in a civil suit or criminal action.

Demurrer — The common law method, still in use in modern courts, by which one party to a civil suit raises the issue of the legal sufficiency of the opposing party's pleading.

Deposition — Testimony of a witness taken outside court as required by law or rule, under oath, and reduced to writing.

Devise — A gift or disposition of real property in a last will and testament.

Diminished Capacity — A partial defense to a criminal charge that does not excuse, but may lessen, the seriousness of the charge.

Directed Verdict — A finding by a trial judge that evidence presented, as a matter of law, requires a decision in favor of one party or the other, without regard to the jury's verdict.

Disbarment — Permanent official suspension of an attorney from the practice of law.

Discharge — The complete removal of liability for debts owed by a debtor filing bankruptcy.

Discovery — A procedure in criminal or civil actions prior to trial in which a party seeks to obtain as much information as possible from the opposing party using depositions, interrogatories, or requests for production of documents or other material evidence.

Divorce — A judicial declaration ending a valid marriage, usually apportioning debts and property and deciding issues of child custody, support, and spousal maintenance.

Divorce, No-Fault — A law allowing courts to grant divorce based on the incompatibility of the spouses, without regard to wrongful conduct, usually requiring a prior period of separation.

Domesticated Animal — See *Animal, Domesticated.*

Domestic Partners — A statutory status granted in some states to unmarried couples living together and providing certain limited property rights to the survivor when one partner dies.

Domicile — A person's permanent legal home.

Double Jeopardy — The prohibition contained in the Fifth Amendment against a person's being tried twice for the same crime, or being tried twice on the basis of the same facts.

Due Process of Law — The guarantee made by the Fifth and Fourteenth Amendments that the rights of a person accused of a crime shall at all times be protected by government and court adherence to prescribed forms of law.

DUI — Driving a motor vehicle "under the influence" of alcohol or drug consumption.

Durable Power of Attorney — See *Power of Attorney, Durable*.

DWI — Driving while intoxicated.

Easement — A right granted by a real property owner to another for limited entrance upon and use of his or her property, such as erection of utility poles or travel on a road necessary to reach an adjacent property.

Embezzlement — The crime of wrongful taking of another's money or property by one to whom it has been entrusted.

Eminent Domain — The power of government to take private property for public use.

Emotional Distress — Suffering psychological injury due to another's wrongful acts, which may be compensable in money damages.

Employee — Any person earning wages, salary, or commissions, not including farm workers, domestic servants, people working for a spouse or parent, railroad employees, and independent contractors.

Entrapment — Any act by a law enforcement officer inducing a person to commit a crime he or she would not otherwise have committed absent that inducement.

Environmental Law — See *Law, Environmental.s*

Equity — A body of judicial rules developed under the common law used to enlarge and protect rights and enforce duties while seeking to avoid unjust constraints and narrowness of statutory law; also, the unrealized value of a person's investment or ownership.

Escrow — The conditional delivery of money or other property to a third person (not the owner) who holds it until the occurrence of a contingent event, then delivers it to the owner.

Estate — Any of various kinds or types of ownership a person may have in real or personal property.

Eviction — The act of depriving a person of possession of real property by process of law, usually used by a landlord against a tenant.

Exemption — The statutory right granted to a debtor in bankruptcy to retain a portion of his or her real or personal property free from a creditor's claims.

Exemption, Homestead — A state statutory exemption of one's home place from creditor claims in bankruptcy.

Express Warranty — See *Warranty*.

Extortion — The crime of obtaining money or property or causing another to act under threat of physical harm or revelation of some damaging fact, usually concerning personal reputation; also called "blackmail."

Extradition — The legal process by which a state governor surrenders a person located within his or her state who is accused or convicted of a crime to authorities in another state where the crime occurred.

Fair Use — The use allowed by law without permission from the copyright holder of copyrighted material in news reporting, critical reviews, comment, teaching, or research.

False Imprisonment — The actionable tort of illegal confinement of a person against his or her will.

Family Partnership — See *Partnership, Family*.

Family Purpose Doctrine — A theory of liability applied in some states holding the head of household owner of a motor vehicle liable for injury caused by any family member driving with permission for pleasure or convenience.

Federal Law — See *Law, Federal*.

Fee Simple Absolute — The highest estate in real property, allowing complete and unrestricted ownership and right to convey title.

Felony — A crime more serious than a misdemeanor, usually punishable by death or a year or more in prison.

Fiduciary — A person holding property in trust for another, as a trustee, guardian, or executor of an estate.

First-Degree Murder — See *Murder*.

Foreman — A jury member chosen to chair jury deliberations and announce a verdict.

Forgery — The crime of making or altering a legally significant writing so as to prejudice the rights of another person.

Fraud — Intentionally misleading actions or false statements known to the maker to be untrue, with knowledge another will rely on the misrepresentation to his or her detriment.

Future Interest — An interest in property, usually real estate, possession and enjoyment of which is delayed until some future time or event.

Gag Order — A judicial order seeking to prevent legal counsel associated with a pending case from making public statements concerning the case, particularly to the news media.

Garnishment — A legal procedure by which money or property due to or owned by one person (the *garnishee*) is taken to pay a debt owed by that person to another person, usually in satisfaction of a court order.

General Power of Attorney — See *Power of Attorney, General*.

Good and Marketable Title — See *Title, Good and Marketable*.

Grantor — A person who conveys real property by deed; also, a person who creates a trust.

Green Card — An identification card issued by the U.S. Immigration and Naturalization Service to legal resident aliens evidencing the right to live and work in the country.

Gross Negligence — See *Negligence, Gross*.

Guardianship — A power conferred on a person (the *guardian*) usually by judicial decree, giving him or her the right and duty to provide personal supervision, care, and control over another person who is unable to care for himself or herself because of some physical or mental disability.

Harassment, Sexual — An actionable statutory tort consisting of unwelcomed sexual advances or offensive remarks or any conduct making an employee's working conditions intolerable, or that cause hostility or intimidation.

Health-Care Power of Attorney — See *Power of Attorney, Medical.*

Hearsay — A usually inadmissible statement made at trial by a witness, based not on personal knowledge, but on what he or she claims to have heard another person say.

Holographic Will — See *Will, Holographic.*

Homestead Exemption — See *Exemption, Homestead.*

Homicide — The crime of one human being's taking the life of another.

Illegitimacy — Denying legal status as a lawful offspring to a child born out of wedlock, a common law rule repealed in most states.

Implied Warranty — See *Warranty.*

Imputed Negligence — See *Negligence, Imputed.*

Incest — The crime of sexual intercourse between blood relatives within the degrees of consanguinity prohibited by state law.

Incorporation — The registration and qualification process by which a corporation is formed under state law.

Incorporation, Articles of — A document filed with an appropriate government agency in order to incorporate a business.

Indemnity — An agreement by which one promises to protect another from any loss or damage, usually describing the role of the insurer in insurance law.

Indenture — A formal contract by which one obligates himself or herself to serve another for a period of time.

Independent Contractor — A person employed by another to do a particular job with a specific result not under the supervision or control of the employer, but strictly under his or her own control until job completion.

Indictment — A formal charge of criminal conduct brought against an individual by a grand jury after investigation.

Informed Consent — Permission given by a patient to a health care provider allowing a recommended treatment after full disclosure of the nature, extent, risks, and probabilities of success and failure of the treatment.

Injunction — A court order commanding or forbidding a person to do a certain act.

Insanity — In a legal sense, an impaired mental condition preventing a person from understanding the nature of his or her actions; or, in some states, a condition suffered by one who understands the nature of his or her actions, but lacks the mental capacity to distinguish right from wrong.

Insurance — A contract (or *policy*) under which a corporation (known as an *insurer*) undertakes to indemnify or pay a person (the *insured*) for a specified loss in return for the insured's payment (a *premium*).

Insurance, No-Fault — A statutory plan in some states under which expenses of personal injury or property damage in a motor vehicle accident are paid by the vehicle owner's insurer without regard to fault.

Intellectual Property — See *Copyright*.

Interest Rate — A charge imposed by a lender on a borrower as payment for money lent or credit extended.

Interrogatories — Written questions submitted by parties to a lawsuit to other parties or potential witnesses, which must be answered truthfully in writing under penalty of perjury.

Intestate — The condition of a person who dies without making a last will and testament, in which case the person's property is distributed to next of kin according to the state law of the deceased's residence.

Invasion of Privacy — A civil tort including unreasonable intrusion into or public disclosure of facts about a person's private life, a false public portrayal of a person, or the unauthorized use of a person's name or picture for commercial purposes without consent.

Involuntary Manslaughter — See *Manslaughter*.

Joint Tenancy — See *Tenancy, Joint*.

Judiciary — The system of federal and state courts.

Judgment — An official and authenticated decision of a court.

Jurisdiction — The statutory authority a court exercises; also, a word used to describe the geographic or subject matter area over which a court has power.

Jury — A statutory number of citizens, usually drawn from voter lists, assembled by state or federal prosecutors to serve as the triers of facts in a civil or criminal trial. A *grand jury* is assembled to decide if sufficient evidence exists to bring an indictment against an accused person.

Jury Selection — The pre-trial questioning of prospective jurors to test each person's qualifications for jury duty, including competency, impartiality, and fairness.

Juvenile Court — A special court trying cases without a jury with jurisdiction over persons under 18 years of age.

Kidnapping — The crime of forcibly abducting, confining, or moving a person against his or her will.

Landlord — The owner (or *lessor*) of real property leased to another (known as the *tenant* or *lessee*).

Larceny — The unlawful taking and carrying away of another's personal property with the intent to permanently deprive the owner thereof.

Last Clear Chance — A theory of comparative negligence applied in some states holding that even though an injured person may have assumed the risk of harm, he or she may recover damages against a defendant who knew of the peril, but failed to act to prevent the harm.

Last Will and Testament — A written document in which a person directs the post mortem distribution of his or her property.

Law, Administrative — The body of law governing hearings, appeals, and other procedures before an agency of government.

Law, Admiralty — The body of specialized law governing maritime commerce and activity.

Law, Common — The large body of law developed in England from judicial decisions based on customs and precedent, constituting the basis of the present U.S. legal system.

Law, Environmental — The body of law protecting and regulating the quality of life, and including prohibitions against pollution of earth, water, and air.

Law, Federal — Any statutory enactment adopted by the U.S. Congress having national authority and application.

Law, Lemon — State law requiring a motor vehicle manufacturer to replace a new car, or refund the purchase price, if the vehicle has major defects.

Lease — A verbal or written contract by which an owner rents real or personal property to a tenant in consideration of periodic payment of rent.

Lease, Commercial — A contract by which the owner (the *lessor*) conveys use and enjoyment of business or professional real estate, equipment, or facilities to another (the *lessee*) for a specific period of time and agreed upon rent.

Leash Law — A local law requiring animals, especially dogs and cats, to be kept on a leash when in public or enclosed in a secure place when at home.

Legacy — See *Bequest*.

Legal Capacity — The competency of parties to make a valid contract, including being at least 18 years of age and of sound mind.

Legislature — The elected body in each state that has the power to make laws for that state.

Lemon Law — See *Law, Lemon*.

Levy — The imposition or collection of an assessment or tax by a government agency, especially the U.S. Internal Revenue Service.

Libel — The actionable tort of writing and publishing a defamatory statement about another person.

Lien — A charge or encumbrance placed on real or personal property preventing transfer of title until the amount owed is paid and the lien removed.

Living Will — See *Advance Directive.*

Loitering — The criminal misdemeanor of remaining or "hanging around" in a public place without apparent purpose.

Loss of Consortium — The compensable loss of a spouse's love, companionship, and services, usually as the result of a tortuous injury.

Mail Fraud — A federal crime of using the U.S. Postal Service as a means to defraud a person of money or property.

Malice Aforethought — The intent to commit a crime or harm another.

Malicious Prosecution — See *Abuse of Process.*

Malpractice — Tortuous, compensable, professional misconduct or lack of professional skill resulting in injury to another.

Manslaughter — The unlawful killing of a person without malice aforethought. *Voluntary manslaughter* is an intentional killing without malice aforethought — *Involuntary manslaughter* is an unintentional killing, usually resulting from criminal negligence.

Marriage — The legal and religious institution whereby a man and woman join in a binding contract for the purpose of founding and maintaining a family. In 2015, the U.S. Supreme Court held that there is a constitutional right for same sex couples to marry.

Marriage, Common Law — The legal status recognized in some states whereby a man and a woman, although not legally wed, intend to marry, treat each other and present themselves to the public as though married, and live together for a minimum period of time, sharing property and earnings.

Mayhem — The crime of intentionally causing bodily harm or disfigurement to another.

Mediation — Intervention between conflicting parties to promote reconciliation, settlement, or compromise, increasingly used as an alternative to the filing of a civil suit.

Medicaid — A joint state and federal health care welfare program, eligibility for which depends on total income and assets, rather than age.

Medical Power of Attorney — See *Power of Attorney, Medical.*

Medicare — A national program of hospital and health care insurance administered by the federal government for people 65 and older and for certain disabled persons, regardless of age.

Minor — Legal description of a person under 18 years of age.

Miranda Warning — The constitutional requirement that police warn any criminal suspect under "custodial interrogation" that the person has the right to remain silent, that statements made can be used against the person, that he or she has the right to a lawyer, and that if he or she cannot afford a lawyer, one will be provided.

Misdemeanor — A criminal act less serious than a felony punishable by fines or short imprisonment.

Mortgage — The legal process by which a buyer or owner of real property (the *mortgagor*) conditionally transfers title to a lender (the *mortgagee*) as security for a loan to finance the purchase of or improvements to the property, the condition being that the transfer becomes void upon full payment or performance according to the stipulated terms.

Money laundering — Concealing the source of illegally gotten money.

Motion to Suppress — A request to the court by defense counsel in a criminal trial to exclude illegally obtained prosecution evidence.

Municipal Ordinance — A law imposed by a county or city government, usually governing a local or regional matter.

Murder — The killing of one human being by another with malice aforethought. *First-degree murder* is a willful and premeditated killing, or killing during the commission of certain felonies, or killing by poison, explosives, or ambush. *Second-degree murder* is an intentional but "spur of the moment" unpremeditated killing, death resulting from an intentional act to do serious bodily harm, or a killing during a lesser felony.

Negligence — The failure of a person to exercise the due care that an ordinary reasonable and prudent person owes others under similar circumstances.

Negligence, Comparative — A theory of tort law in which liability for negligence and the payment of consequent damages are apportioned between the parties involved in a negligent act, based on the culpability of each.

Negligence, Contributory — A negligent act or omission by an injured party contributing to that party's own injury.

Negligence, Gross — An extreme form of negligence in which a person or other legal entity acts with total reckless disregard of the consequences, thereby seriously injuring another.

Negligence, Imputed — A legal theory transferring to one person legal responsibility for the negligence of another, usually between a negligent employee and his or her employer, or a child and parent.

Negotiable Instrument — Any written evidence of ownership of money or property, title to which is capable of being transferred from one person by delivery to another with or without endorsement, such as a promissory note or check.

No-Fault Divorce — See *Divorce, No-Fault.*

No-Fault Insurance — See *Insurance, No-Fault.*

Nolo Contendere — Latin for "I will not contest," a plea to a criminal charge having the legal consequences of admitting guilt, but which may not be used as evidence of guilt or liability elsewhere.

Nondischargeable Debt — A debt in bankruptcy that by law cannot be forgiven, including alimony, child support, government educational loans, and taxes owed for a period of three years or less before filing bankruptcy.

Obstruction of Justice — A crime committed when a person attempts to convince, bribe, or intimidate a witness or a victim not to testify against an accused.

Offer — A written or verbal promise by one person (the *offeror*) to another (the *offeree*) to do or not to do some future act, usually in exchange for a mutual promise.

Parole — Conditional release of a criminal prisoner under federal or state supervision for the balance of his or her sentence.

Partnership — An association of two or more persons formed to conduct business for mutual profit.

Partnership, Family — A legal business relationship created by agreement among two or more family members for a common purpose, often used as a means to transfer income and assets among family members so as to limit individual personal liability and taxes.

Partnership, Limited — A partnership in which individuals known as *limited partners* have no management role, but receive periodic income and are personally liable for partnership debts only to the extent of their individual investments.

Patent — Official government registration giving an inventor exclusive rights to make, use, and sell an invention.

PATRIOT Act — A U.S. law enacted in response to the September 11, 2001 terrorist attacks, which gave law-enforcement officials greater ability to tap telephones and track Internet users; also called "The Uniting and Strengthening America by Providing Appropriate Tools Required to Intercept and Obstruct Terrorism Act of 2001."

Periodic Tenancy — See *Tenancy, Periodic*.

Perjury — The crime of willfully lying under oath.

Personal Property — See *Property*.

Petty Offense — A misdemeanor crime usually punishable by six months or less in jail.

Plaintiff — The initiating party who complains of a wrong in a civil suit.

Plea Bargain — A way of avoiding a criminal trial in which the state drops or reduces charges or recommends a reduced sentence in exchange for a defendant's agreement to plead guilty or to give evidence against others, subject to the approval of the court.

Pocket Part — A pamphlet inserted in the back of bound law books annually, updating changes in law and adding court decisions.

Policy — In insurance law, the contract between the insurer and the insured.

Polygraph — The mechanical instrument known as a "lie detector" test, designed to measure a person's truthfulness based on physical reactions to questions.

Power of Attorney — A document that authorizes a named person to act on behalf of the signer.

Power of Attorney, Durable — A power of attorney that remains in effect even when the person who signed it becomes incompetent.

Power of Attorney, General — A power of attorney that conveys almost unlimited right to deal with the signer's assets.

Power of Attorney, Medical (or Health-Care) — A power of attorney that is limited to decisions about medical treatment when the signer is unable to make such decisions.

Precedent — The concept that law announced in prior court decisions governs subsequent judicial cases on the same issue.

Premarital Agreement — See *Agreement, Premarital*.

Privileged Communications — Certain communications protected by state law and inadmissible as evidence, usually between a person and his or her attorney, doctor, psychiatrist, or religious adviser.

Probable Cause — A standard of evidence required for police to obtain a search warrant, meaning reasonable grounds for the belief in alleged facts, slightly more firm than mere suspicion but including rumor, gossip, or even a hunch.

Probate — A series of court proceedings initially determining the validity of a last will and testament, then supervising the administration or execution of the terms of the will.

Probation — Allowing one convicted of a crime to go free with a suspended sentence due to good behavior.

Promissory Estoppel — The legal rule barring one who makes a promise from reneging once the party to whom it was made has acted on the promise to his or her detriment.

Property — Anything of value capable of being owned, including land (*real property*) and *personal property*, both tangible and intangible.

Prostitution — The misdemeanor crime of engaging in sexual activity in exchange for money.

Proximate Cause — In tort cases, any foreseeable injury-producing act or omission which in the ordinary course of events, unbroken by any intervening cause, produces an injury, and without which the injury would not have occurred.

Punitive Damages — See *Damages*.

Quitclaim Deed — See *Deed, Quitclaim*.

Rape — The crime of a person having sexual intercourse with another person without their consent, usually involving force. Statutory rape is sexual intercourse with a person under a statutory age, with or without their consent.

Reaffirmation — A statement filed in bankruptcy in which a debtor voluntarily waives the right to the discharge of certain debts.

Real Estate — Land and anything growing or erected thereon or permanently attached thereto.

Real Property — See *Property*.

Reasonable Person — In tort law, an average adult of unspecified age without physical or mental disabilities, who is cautious without being excessively careful.

Redemption — The statutory right allowed a mortgagor whose mortgage has been foreclosed to regain title to the subject property by paying all payments in arrears.

Registrar of Wills — A county government official in some states whose duty is to accept and file a testator's last will and testament, then index and maintain the will in private for post mortem reference by heirs.

Relevancy — The rule requiring that to be admissible, evidence must relate to a material issue in the case.

Replevin — The common law procedural form of action filed in court by a person seeking return of his or her personal property held by another.

Reporter Series — Official published books containing reports of federal and state court decisions.

Restrictive Covenant — Restriction in a real property deed preventing a certain described use, such as residential or commercial use or the keeping of animals.

Right of Survivorship — An attribute of a joint tenancy that automatically transfers ownership of the share of a deceased joint tenant to surviving joint tenants without the necessity of probate.

Robbery — The crime of taking money or property from another person against his or her will by force or intimidation.

Sanction — A money fine or other punishment for misconduct imposed by a court, usually on an attorney.

Search Warrant — A document obtained by police from a judge or magistrate based on probable cause authorizing the search of a described premises to determine if specific evidence of a crime exists.

Second-Degree Murder — See *Murder*.

Security Deposit — A sum of money paid by a lessee to a landlord as security for damages to the premises, varying in amount by custom in different geographic areas, usually refundable at lease termination.

Self Defense — The right of a person to use all reasonable force to protect himself or herself or a companion when physically attacked or in immediate danger of harm from another person.

Separation — The cessation of a husband and wife's living together by mutual agreement or by judicial decree, often as a prelude to a divorce.

Separation Agreement — See *Agreement, Separation*.

Settlement — In real estate sales, a final meeting of seller, buyer, the lender financing the purchase, and the real estate agent at which necessary documents are signed, including the deed and mortgage, and payment is made.

Settlor — See *Grantor*.

Sexual Harassment — See *Harassment, Sexual*.

Slander — Spoken words defaming another person's character.

Small Claims Court — A local county or city court in which civil cases involving money claims up to a statutory maximum are filed, litigated, and decided by a judge without a jury under simplified procedures with the parties representing themselves.

Social Security — The national system providing federal old-age, disability, and unemployment benefits paid out of a trust fund to which employers and employees are required by law to contribute.

Sole Proprietorship — The conduct of an unincorporated business when an individual owns all business assets and is personally liable for all debts and obligations.

Solicitation — The crime of requesting another person to commit a crime or to assist in committing a crime.

Sovereign Immunity — An ancient legal doctrine still in effect that exempts the government from lawsuits filed by citizens unless the government waives that immunity and allows the litigation.

Special Damages — See *Damages*.

Specific Performance — A remedy for breach of contract in which a court orders a party at fault to carry out the contract terms.

Spendthrift Trust — See *Trust, Spendthrift*.

Squatter's Rights — See *Adverse Possession*.

Statutes — The official published version of federal or state laws. *Annotated statutes* also contain references to judicial decisions interpreting various laws.

Statute of Limitations — A statutory period of years after the expiration of which a person cannot be charged with a crime.

Statutory Rape — See *Rape*.

Stream of Commerce — A theory allowing a party injured by a product to sue the product manufacturer, distributor, wholesaler, and/or the retail sales outlet where it was purchased.

Strict Liability — The theory that a manufacturer owes a general duty to any person who may use a product to make the product so that it may be used safely and without any inherent defects.

Subchapter "S" Corporation — *See Corporation, Subchapter 'S'*.

Subpoena — A court order commanding the appearance of a person or the production of documents or other material named in the subpoena.

Summary Judgment — A motion in a civil trial seeking a ruling on the basis there is no material dispute of fact and, as a matter of law, the moving party has a right to a favorable judgment.

Summons — An initial document served in a civil suit or a criminal misdemeanor case informing the defendant of the nature of the cause, his or her rights, and the procedure for filing a response.

Supreme Court — The highest federal court, the final arbiter of the meaning of the U.S. Constitution and all laws.

Tax Lien — A lien placed on property by the IRS or state tax authority for unpaid taxes.

Tenancy By the Entireties — A joint tenancy between husband and wife, with the right of survivorship.

Tenancy, Joint — A form of property co-ownership in which parties hold equal title with the right of survivorship.

Tenancy, Periodic — A short lease between a landlord and tenant, usually for weekly or monthly occupancy.

Glossary

Time Share — A form of joint multiple ownership by contract in which an undivided interest in vacation property is purchased, each co-owner having an assigned time period of use.

Title, Good and Marketable — A real property seller's guarantee that no legal defects or other encumbrances impair his or her title to the property, as evidenced by a title search of official public land and tax records.

Tort — A "wrong" committed against a person or a person's property in which a duty of due care exists, the duty is breached, and the result is an injury that may serve as the basis for a civil suit.

Trademark — A registered and legally protected distinctive mark, symbol, or device a manufacturer affixes to a product to identify it for the buying public.

Trade Secret — A process, device, or formula used in business that is not divulged to the public.

Traffic Violation — Any breach of the motor vehicle code or related laws.

Treason — A serious constitutional crime consisting of an attempt to overthrow the federal or a state government by force or violence, the punishment for which can be death.

Trespass to Chattels — Unlawful damage to, or interference with, another's personal property.

Trespass to Real Property — Intrusion upon another's real property without justification or permission.

Trust — A legal device allowing title to and possession of property to be held, used, and/or managed by one person (the *trustee*) for the benefit of others (the **beneficiaries**).

Trust, Spendthrift — A restricted trust created to pay income to a beneficiary judged by the trust settlor to be too improvident to handle his or her own personal economic affairs.

Unemployment Compensation — Benefits paid by the government to persons unable to find work.

Uninsured Motorist Fund — A state fund used to pay persons injured by motorists who have no auto insurance coverage.

United States Constitution — See *Constitution, United States.*

Venue — The geographic place in which a trial takes place.

Voluntary Manslaughter — See *Manslaughter.*

Ward — A minor child for whom a court has appointed a guardian.

Warranty — A promise that a statement is true, usually by a manufacturer or seller of a commercial product. An *express warranty* is created by explicit statements. An *implied warranty* is inferred by law from the nature of the transaction.

Warranty Deed — See *Deed, Warranty.*

Will — See *Last Will and Testament.*

Will, Holographic — A will written in the handwriting of the testator.

Will, Living — See *Advance Directive.*

Workman's Compensation — Federal and state funds paid to workers injured on the job.

Zoning — Laws imposed on the use of real property, as when land in designated areas is restricted exclusively to residential or commercial use.